What's
on your
Mind?

Discover the Power of Biblical Thinking

John Goetsch

Striving Together Publications
4020 E. Lancaster Blvd.
Lancaster, CA 93535
800.201.7748

Cover design by Andrew Jones
Layout by Craig Parker
Edited by Cary Schmidt and Maggie Ruhl
Special thanks to our proofreaders.

ISBN 978-1-59894-103-6

Printed in the United States of America

Table of Contents

How to Use This Curriculum

Take a moment to familiarize yourself with the features of this *Striving Together* Sunday school curriculum:

Schedule

The lessons contained in this curriculum are undated, allowing you to begin and end the teaching series at any time. There are thirteen lessons that may be taught weekly any time of the year.

Student Edition Books

Companion books are available through *Striving Together Publications*. These contain:

- The outlines with blanks that students may fill in during the lessons

- Various Scripture quotations that are used throughout each lesson
- The introductory lesson overviews
- Study questions for review throughout the week
- A suggested memory verse for each lesson

These books are excellent tools for the members of a class. We suggest ordering enough books for each member of the class, plus additional copies for new members who enroll in the class throughout the teaching series. Giving class members a study book encourages faithfulness to the class, provides students with a devotional tool for use throughout the week, and allows them to review what they learned previously.

Key Verses

The verses from which the lessons are taken are included at the beginning of each lesson. These are provided so that you may read them through several times in prayerful preparation for your time in class. Many teachers choose to memorize their key verses. During the class hour, we suggest that you use your own Bible for Scripture reading and encourage your class members to do so as well.

Lesson Summary and Lesson Aim

The summary and aim sections are provided so that you may be aware of the overall emphasis of each lesson, especially as they relate to the other lessons in the curriculum. These brief statements provide a snapshot of where each lesson will take the students.

Lesson Goals

Bible teaching has a higher goal than the delivery of information. That goal is a life changed. Students want to know what they are to do with what they are given from God's Word. As you prepare for and teach each lesson, emphasize how those listening may apply its truths throughout the week.

Teaching Outline

The abbreviated outline enables you to view the entire lesson at a glance to see how the content fits together. Teaching with an organized outline increases the students' abilities to understand and remember the lesson content.

The Created Mind

Key Verses

ISAIAH 55:8–9

8   *For my thoughts are not your thoughts, neither are your ways my ways, saith the LORD.*
9   *For as the heavens are higher than the earth, so are my ways higher than your ways, and my thoughts than your thoughts.*

Lesson Summary

The fascinating and complex human mind points to the evidence of its Creator. This lesson reveals how a designed creation under divine control has the capacity to make choices that lead to a successful, God-fulfilled life.

Lesson Aim

To fundamentally prove that God is the designer of the mind, and His creation is designed to glorify Him.

Lesson Goals

At the conclusion of this lesson, students should:

1.   Understand that God is the great designer of the mind.
2.   Realize that out of all creation, only man can choose to accept or deny God.
3.   Know the difference between temptation and sin.

4. Know that our minds were created to make choices to glorify God.

Teaching Outline

    I. Our Minds Are Designed Creations
        A. Created by the Father
        B. Calling for our faith

    II. Our Minds Are under a Divine Control
        A. A limited mind
        B. A limitless mind

    III. Our Minds Can Make Deliberate Choices
        A. A choice to reverence
        B. A chance to run

The Created Mind

Text

...ll received the word w/readyness of mind "

ACTS 17:24–28

24 God that made the world and all things therein, seeing that he is Lord of heaven and earth, dwelleth not in temples made with hands;

25 Neither is worshipped with men's hands, as though he needed any thing, seeing he giveth to all life, and breath, and all things;

26 And hath made of one blood all nations of men for to dwell on all the face of the earth, and hath determined the times before appointed, and the bounds of their habitation;

27 That they should seek the Lord, if haply they might feel after him, and find him, though he be not far from every one of us:

28 For in him we live, and move, and have our being; as certain also of your own poets have said, For we are also his offspring.

Introduction

No computer can or ever will match the ability of the human brain. Our minds have an amazing capacity to receive, store, and process information at unbelievable speeds and in unparalleled amounts.

> **TEACHING TIP**
>
> *Consider researching "the brain versus the computer" and share facts with your class about how the brain is unquestionably more advanced.*

I. Our Minds Are Designed Creations

A. Created by the Father

The architect and creator of all things is God Himself. *"All things were made by him; and without him was not any thing made that was made"* (John 1:3). The "self-made" man does not exist! *"A man can receive nothing, except it be given him from heaven"* (John 3:27). Man boasts of his knowledge and skill, but without God, we can do nothing. *"For who maketh thee to differ from another? and what hast thou that thou didst not receive? now if thou didst receive it, why dost thou glory, as if thou hadst not received it?"* (1 Corinthians 4:7).

[handwritten margin note: Name of God]

B. Calling for our faith

It takes a great amount of faith to be an evolutionist. To believe that we evolved over billions of years from a tiny amoeba that was floating in water takes a lot of faith (of course we have not yet explained where the water came from, or the planet on which the water existed). There

4

are just too many gaps in the evolution theory that must be filled with enormous faith to believe it. It would be a lot easier to believe by faith the words of the psalmist, *"By the word of the LORD were the heavens made; and all the host of them by the breath of his mouth. He gathereth the waters of the sea together as an heap: he layeth up the depth in storehouses. Let all the earth fear the LORD: let all the inhabitants of the world stand in awe of him. For he spake, and it was done; he commanded, and it stood fast"* (Psalm 33:6–9).

Perhaps the most intricate of all creations is the human body.

PSALM 139:13–17
13   For thou hast possessed my reins: thou hast covered me in my mother's womb.
14   I will praise thee; for I am fearfully and wonderfully made: marvellous are thy works; and that my soul knoweth right well.
15   My substance was not hid from thee, when I was made in secret, and curiously wrought in the lowest parts of the earth.
16   Thine eyes did see my substance, yet being unperfect; and in thy book all my members were written, which in continuance were fashioned, when as yet there was none of them.
17   How precious also are thy thoughts unto me, O God! how great is the sum of them!

Paul begins his address to those on Mars' Hill by saying, *"God that made the world and all things therein, seeing that he is Lord of heaven and earth, dwelleth not in temples made with hands; Neither is worshipped with men's hands, as though he needed any thing, seeing he giveth to all life, and breath, and all things"* (Acts 17:24–25). Our bodies and minds are **Designed Creations**.

II. Our Minds Are under a Divine Control

A. *A limited mind*

As part of God's creation, we are not in charge! The minds that God has created within us have astounding capabilities, but they are limited. Only God is omniscient. We are limited in our knowledge because God has placed a boundary on our minds. *"The secret things belong unto the LORD our God: but those things which are revealed belong unto us and to our children for ever, that we may do all the words of this law"* (Deuteronomy 29:29). While man has accumulated information for centuries so that we as individuals do not have to learn everything from scratch, God still declares, *"For my thoughts are not your thoughts, neither are your ways my ways, saith the LORD. For as the heavens are higher than the earth, so are my ways higher than your ways, and my thoughts than your thoughts"* (Isaiah 55:8–9).

B. *A limitless mind*

Paul reminds these intellectuals that God *"hath made of one blood all nations of men for to dwell on the face of the earth, and hath determined the times before appointed, and the **bounds of their habitation**"* [Emphasis mine] (Acts 17:26). When I hear of the development of science in areas like cloning, I wonder if we are getting close to the boundary that God has set for our minds. There are many things that God knows are best for us not to know. Don't let what you can't understand weaken your faith.

I can't humanly explain the eternal being of God. I can't put into human terms the fact that God had no beginning but has always existed. This concept is impossible for me to fathom, but my inability to explain it makes it no less true. That's where faith enters the equation.

One day our faith will become sight! *"For now we see through a glass, darkly; but then face to face: now I know in part; but then shall I know even as also I am known"* (1 Corinthians 13:12). Our good God has placed **A Divine Control** upon our minds.

III. Our Minds Can Make Deliberate Choices

A. A choice to reverence

Along with the ability of our minds to receive, process, and store information, God has given us the ability to make choices about that information. Paul reminds the audience that they have a choice about whom they will worship. *"That they should seek the Lord, if haply they might feel after him, and find him, though he be not far from every one of us. For in him we live, and move, and have our being; as certain also of your own poets have said, For we are also his offspring"* (Acts 17:27–28).

B. A chance to run

Animals are created with an instinctive reflex—they don't think before they react. If you pull a dog's ears, he may bite you, because he is simply reacting to an adverse stimuli. The human brain however has the ability to pause between stimuli and response so that a right choice can be made. God has created a "buffer" between the stimulus and the response.

Illustration

Scientists have been studying the brain for years, and while there is much to learn, here is what they say about the human mind's capability of choice: "Neuronal activity begins in the sensory areas of the brain for as much as a second before voluntary motor activity occurs. Also, neuronal activity begins in the premotor areas of the cortex and in some areas of the basal ganglia many milliseconds before motor activity occurs in the motor cortex. Therefore, it is currently thought that cerebration occurring in these integrative portions of the brain, operating in association with the cerebellum, conceives and plans the complex sequence of movements that is to be executed. Only after the plan has been established is the primary motor system set into action to cause the sequential movements" (Arthur C. Guyton, *Human Physiology and Mechanisms of Disease*, Philadelphia, W.B. Saunders Company, 1987, p. 413).

This is why we come to understand that to be tempted is not sin—even Jesus *"was in all points tempted like as we are, yet without sin"* (Hebrews 4:15). In other words, the same wrong stimuli that calls to us every day, likewise tempted our Saviour. But in that moment of choice, He did not sin—for He was God. In that split second of time between temptation and response, our minds have the ability to choose. Think about the following two stories from Scripture. In both cases there was temptation, but the choices made were very different.

GENESIS 3:1–6

1   *Now the serpent was more subtil than any beast of the field which the LORD God had made. And he said unto the woman, Yea, hath God said, Ye shall not eat of every tree of the garden?*

2   *And the woman said unto the serpent, We may eat of the fruit of the trees of the garden:*

3   *But of the fruit of the tree which is in the midst of the garden, God hath said, Ye shall not eat of it, neither shall ye touch it, lest ye die.*

4   *And the serpent said unto the woman, Ye shall not surely die:*

5   *For God doth know that in the day ye eat thereof, then your eyes shall be opened, and ye shall be as gods, knowing good and evil.*

6   *And when the woman saw that the tree was good for food, and that it was pleasant to the eyes, and a tree to be desired to make one wise, she took of the fruit thereof, and did eat, and gave also unto her husband with her; and he did eat.*

GENESIS 39:7–10

7   *And it came to pass after these things, that his master's wife cast her eyes upon Joseph; and she said, Lie with me.*

8   *But he refused, and said unto his master's wife, Behold, my master wotteth not what is with me in the house, and he hath committed all that he hath to my hand;*

9   *There is none greater in this house than I; neither hath he kept back any thing from me but thee, because thou art his wife: how then can I do this great wickedness, and sin against God?*

10   *And it came to pass, as she spake to Joseph day by day, that he hearkened not unto her, to lie by her, or to be with her.*

What a difference a simple choice made in these lives. Both were tempted (that wasn't the sin), but it was what they did with that temptation that made the difference between right and wrong. We are not simply "products of our environment" as Sigmund Freud and Carl Rogers would have us believe, nor are we simply conditioned in our behavior by stimuli as B.F. Skinner and others would teach. We are products of our choices conceived in our minds and carried out in our actions. No one can make us do wrong without our consent. Solomon of old understood well the power of choices and advised his son, "...*if sinners entice thee, consent thou not*" (Proverbs 1:10).

Conclusion

The human mind—what a fascinating work of God! It is a **Designed Creation** under **Divine Control** with an ability to make **Deliberate Choices.** It would be wise for us to daily ask our Creator to "*Let the words of my mouth, and the meditation of my heart, be acceptable in thy sight, O LORD, my strength and my redeemer*" (Psalm 19:14).

Study Questions

1. Who is the creator of your mind? See John 1:3.
   God is the creator of the mind.

2. What is the most intricate of all creations? See Psalm 139:13–17.
   Each individual is the most intricate of all creations.

3. In a split second of time between temptation and response, our minds have the ability to make a choice. Compare and contrast the following stories in the Bible: Eve and the serpent (Genesis 3:1–6) and Joseph (Genesis 39:7–10). How were their responses to temptation different? Were their temptations similar?
   When Eve was tempted by the serpent, she chose to listen to her fleshly desire to have the wisdom of gods—knowing good and evil. This choice led her to be deceived, which in return led her to tempt Adam. On the other hand, when Joseph was tempted, he determined that allowing his flesh to prevail would mean sinning against God. He chose to flee temptation.

4. God has placed boundaries on your mind—your knowledge and understanding. Do you find yourself trusting your logic—your limited mind—instead of God's omniscience? List five areas in your life in which you need to trust God.
   Answers may vary.

5. Write out the wise counsel David gave to his son in 1 Chronicles 28:9.
   "And thou, Solomon my son, know thou the God of thy father, and serve him with a perfect heart and with

a willing mind: for the LORD searcheth all hearts, and understandeth all the imaginations of the thoughts: if thou seek him, he will be found of thee; but if thou forsake him, he will cast thee off for ever."—1 CHRONICLES 28:9

6. Ken Collier once said, "Only two choices on the shelf: pleasing God or pleasing self." What five choices can you make this week that will please and glorify God? *Answers may vary.*

7. Proverbs 1:10 shows you when to make a particular choice, and it even tells you the right choice to make. Write out this verse.
"My son, if sinners entice thee, consent thou not." —PROVERBS 1:10

8. Spend time every day this week asking the Creator to *"Let the words of my mouth, and the meditation of my heart, be acceptable in thy sight, O LORD, my strength and my redeemer"* (Psalm 19:14). *Responses may vary.*

Memory Verses

"For my thoughts are not your thoughts, neither are your ways my ways, saith the LORD. For as the heavens are higher than the earth, so are my ways higher than your ways, and my thoughts than your thoughts."—ISAIAH 55:8–9

The Changed Mind

Key Verses

LAMENTATIONS 3:22–23

22 *It is of the* LORD'*s mercies that we are not consumed, because his compassions fail not.*

23 *They are new every morning: great is thy faithfulness.*

Lesson Summary

Paul challenges the thinking of those who were gathered on Mars' Hill. While they were being open-minded to the pluralistic thinking of their day, Paul admonished them to "change their minds"—stop looking to lifeless idols and start looking to the living God. This lesson penetrates right to the heart of the matter and focuses on establishing a solid relationship with God.

Lesson Aim

To place ourselves in a relationship with a living God, for when we do, we'll quickly see the need for a changed mind.

Lesson Goals

At the conclusion of this lesson, students should:

1. Take inventory of their lives—looking for any lifeless idols they have been serving.
2. Realize that God is just as much alive now as He was on Mars' Hill.

3. Understand that God is a God of second, third, and fourth chances—He is longsuffering.
4. Desire to repent of any unconfessed sin so that they may draw closer to the Lord.

Teaching Outline

   I. He Presents a Living God
     A. The ruse of lifeless gods
     B. The reality of a living God

  II. He Presents a Longsuffering God
     A. A God of compassion
     B. A God of chances

 III. He Presents a Lawful God
     A. A call for repentance
     B. A challenge to revolutionize

The Changed Mind

Text

ACTS 17:29–30

29 Forasmuch then as we are the offspring of God, we ought not to think that the Godhead is like unto gold, or silver, or stone, graven by art and man's device.

30 And the times of this ignorance God winked at; but now commandeth all men every where to repent:

Introduction

Paul now begins to challenge the thinking of those who were gathered there on Mars' Hill. While they were very open-minded to the pluralistic thinking of their day, Paul admonishes them to "change their minds." *"Forasmuch then as we are the offspring of God, we **ought not to think** that the Godhead is like unto gold, or silver, or stone, graven* *by art and man's device. And the times of this ignorance God winked at; but now commandeth all men every where to repent"* [Emphasis mine] (Acts 17:29–30). Their thinking about God was wrong and needed to be changed. That wrong thinking is a result of the sin nature.

Not only are we born sinners, we are born with a sin nature. That is, our very being or makeup is sinful. Thus, not only do we do wrong things naturally, we think wrong things naturally. *"And you hath he quickened, who were dead in trespasses and sins; Wherein in time past ye walked according to the course of this world, according to the prince of the power of the air, the spirit that now worketh in the children of disobedience: Among whom also we all had our conversation in times past in the lusts of our flesh, fulfilling the desires of the flesh **and of the mind**; and were by nature the children of wrath, even as others"* [Emphasis mine] (Ephesians 2:1–3). A man in his natural sinful state does sinful things, but he also thinks sinfully, because his mind is sinful. *"Unto the pure all things are pure: but unto them that are defiled and unbelieving is nothing pure; **but even their mind and conscience is defiled**"* [Emphasis mine] (Titus 1:15). We often focus on the lifestyle that needs to change at salvation, but conversion also involves a changed mind. (Interestingly, the word *repentance* simply means "a change of mind.")

It is natural to think we are doing okay until we meet someone doing better. Never is this more evident than when we come face to face with God! *"In the year that king Uzziah died I saw also the Lord sitting upon a throne, high and lifted up, and his train filled the temple.... Then said I, Woe is me! for I am undone; because I am a man of unclean lips, and I dwell in the midst of a people of unclean lips: for mine eyes have seen the King, the LORD of hosts"* (Isaiah 6:1, 5). *"If I had not come and spoken unto them, they had not had sin: but now they have no cloak for their sin"* (John 15:22). Paul pulls the cloak from off their wrong thinking by presenting the "unknown" God to them.

I. He Presents a Living God

A. The ruse of lifeless gods

"*Forasmuch then as we are the offspring of God, we ought not to think that the Godhead is like unto gold, or silver, or stone, graven by art and man's device*" (Acts 17:29). While the altars on Mars' Hill were beautifully carved and adorned, they all had one thing in common. They were all lifeless! Paul says, "You've been thinking all wrong. Let me introduce you to Someone who is alive!" Jeremiah says, "*But the LORD is the true God, he is the living God, and an everlasting king*" (Jeremiah 10:10). The gods of this world offer no hope, for they have no life. Man is looking for peace, joy, fulfillment, and contentment, but it will never be found in stone statues or golden figurines. The sinful nature leaves man's soul parched and dry, and as the psalmist, he cries, "*My soul thirsteth for God, for the living God*" [Emphasis mine] (Psalm 42:2).

B. The reality of a living God

On a gloomy day in Bethany, Jesus stood in a graveyard. All around him the sobbing of those grieving could be heard, because they had felt the sting of death once again. But the imps of Hell trembled when the Son of God lifted His voice above the cloud of despair and cried, "*I am the resurrection, and the life: he that believeth in me, though he were dead, yet shall he live: And whosoever liveth and believeth in me shall never die*" (John 11:25–26).

King Darius changed his mind about **the living God.** Regrettably, the king had allowed his entourage to trick him into signing a decree that was sure to send Daniel to a den of lions. The writing was signed and could not be changed *"according to the law of the Medes and the Persians, which altereth not"* (Daniel 6:8). The king knew he had made a mistake, yet he had no choice but to put Daniel into that lions' den. But that's not the end of the story!

DANIEL 6:17–22, 24–27

17 And a stone was brought, and laid upon the mouth of the den; and the king sealed it with his own signet, and with the signet of his lords; that the purpose might not be changed concerning Daniel.

18 Then the king went to his palace, and passed the night fasting: neither were instruments of musick brought before him: and his sleep went from him.

19 Then the king arose very early in the morning, and went in haste unto the den of lions.

20 And when he came to the den, he cried with a lamentable voice unto Daniel: and the king spake and said to Daniel, O Daniel, __servant of the living God__, is thy God, whom thou servest continually, able to deliver thee from the lions?

21 Then said Daniel unto the king, O king, live for ever.

22 My God hath sent his angel, and hath shut the lions' mouths, that they have not hurt me: forasmuch as before him innocency was found in me; and also before thee, O king, have I done no hurt.

24 And the king commanded, and they brought those men which had accused Daniel, and they cast them into the den of lions, them, their children, and their wives; and the lions had the mastery of them, and brake all their bones in pieces or ever they came at the bottom of the den.

25 Then king Darius wrote unto all people, nations, and languages, that dwell in all the earth; Peace be multiplied unto you.

26 I make a decree, That in every dominion of my kingdom men tremble and fear before the God of Daniel: **for he is the living God,** *and stedfast for ever, and his kingdom that which shall not be destroyed, and his dominion shall be even unto the end.*

27 He delivereth and rescueth, and he worketh signs and wonders in heaven and in earth, who hath delivered Daniel from the power of the lions. [Emphasis mine]

What gods are you trusting in to deliver you? Will your idol of money, power, or sex deliver you from the power of sin and death? It's time to change your mind! We need people today like those in Thessalonica who *"...turned to God from idols to serve* **the living and true God***"* [Emphasis mine] (1 Thessalonians 1:9).

II. He Presents a Longsuffering God

A. A God of compassion

"And the times of this ignorance God winked at" (Acts 17:30). God could have made all of those altars on Mars' Hill fall over. (The god Dagon had a little trouble staying on his feet back in the Old Testament.) But God is a patient, longsuffering God. *"It is of the* LORD's *mercies that we are not consumed, because his compassions fail not. They are new every morning: great is thy faithfulness"* (Lamentations 3:22–23).

B. A God of chances

Aren't you glad that God is a God of second chances? It has been said that the average person hears the Gospel forty times before he gets saved! What a patient God. *"The LORD is merciful and gracious, slow to anger, and plenteous in mercy"* (Psalm 103:8).

TEACHING TIP

Think about a time or find a story of when God gave someone a second chance. Share it with the class.

God is so unlike us. We are not very quick to give someone a second chance, much less a third, fourth, or fortieth chance! If you and I were God, Heaven would be empty. But, *"The Lord is not slack concerning his promise, as some men count slackness; **but is longsuffering** to usward, not willing that any should perish, but that all should come to repentance"* [Emphasis mine] (2 Peter 3:9). In fact, *"Who is a God like unto thee, that pardoneth iniquity, and passeth by the transgression of the remnant of his heritage? he retaineth not his anger for ever, **because he delighteth in mercy**"* [Emphasis mine] (Micah 7:18). The longsuffering of God ought to be enough to change anyone's mind.

Our God is **A Living God** and **A Longsuffering God**, but then...

III. He Presents a Lawful God

A. A call for repentance

Don't get too comfortable with God's patience. He has winked at this ignorance, *"...but now commandeth all men every where to repent"* (Acts 17:30). Notice this is not a suggestion; it is a command! And it's for all men—everywhere! It is not just for the reprobate, but for the religious. It is not just for the one who sits in prison, but for the one who sits in the pews.

Ever since the first sin, man has followed Adam's example of blaming his sin on others, rationalizing it away and finding some kind of man-made fig leaves to cover it up. Sin is not judged by the way *we* see it, but by the way *God* sees it. Sin is not on the judgment stand here; the sinner is! God is not speaking to the *sin,* but to the *sinner.* The problem is not in the *deed* of sin; it is in the *doer of the deed.* Sin isn't going to change, but we as sinners must. *"Repent therefore of this thy wickedness, and pray God, if perhaps **the thought of thine heart** may be forgiven thee"* [Emphasis mine] (Acts 8:22).

B. A challenge to revolutionize

Too often, man changes his actions when he gets caught, but never changes his mind about sin. In fact, to most people today, it's not sin unless you get caught! For sure, it is our actions that remind us that there is a problem of sin and we need to stop. But notice how God's instructions about repentance go beyond the actions, *"...Repent, and turn yourselves from all your transgressions; so iniquity shall not be your ruin. Cast away from you all your transgressions, whereby ye have transgressed; and make you **a new heart** and **a new spirit**: for why will ye die, O house of Israel?"* [Emphasis mine] (Ezekiel 18:30–31).

Conclusion

Nothing will change as long as we compare ourselves with the status quo of humanity. We probably stack up pretty well compared to the majority, but to do so is a huge mistake. *"For we dare not make ourselves of the number, or compare ourselves with some that commend themselves: but they measuring themselves by themselves, and comparing themselves among themselves, are not wise"* (2 Corinthians 10:12). We must place ourselves next to **A Living God, A Longsuffering God,** and **A Lawful God.** When we do, we'll quickly see the need for *A Changed Mind.*

Study Questions

1. Write out the words that describe God in Psalm 103:8.
    The words that describe God in Psalm 103:8 are: merciful,
    gracious, slow to anger, and plenteous in mercy.

2. What does God command of every man in Acts 17:30?
    God commands of every man to repent.

3. How does the story of Daniel in the lions' den prove the
    fact that a living God does exist? See Daniel 6:18–27.
    When Daniel was faced with a life-threatening
    circumstance, he believed in his God, and God proved
    that He was alive and real when He chose to save Daniel
    from the lions because of his belief.

4. Ezekiel 18:30 says, "*…Repent, and turn yourselves from*
    all your transgressions; so iniquity shall not be your
    ruin." Write down the sins with which you struggle
    most. Review this list and repent of your sins to your
    Heavenly Father. Then, explain how you plan to turn
    from these transgressions the next time Satan tries to
    tempt you with them.
    Answers may vary.

5. Write out the command of repentance in Acts 8:22.
    "Repent therefore of this thy wickedness, and pray God, if
    perhaps the thought of thine heart may be forgiven thee."
    —Acts 8:22

6. What gods do you trust to deliver you? Do you
    find yourself relying on money, power, success, or
    relationships to fulfill your needs in life more than

you do the God of Heaven? How can 1 Thessalonians 1:9 challenge you to put your trust in the right place?
Answers may vary.

7.   When answering to a lawful God, the problem isn't the deed of sin; the problem lies with the doer of the deed. Read Ezekiel 18:30–31 and summarize the truths found in these verses as they relate to repentance of sin.
God will judge us according to the way in which we live. With this truth in mind, for sin not to be the ruler in our lives, we need to repent and turn from our sinful habits. Not only do we need to turn from our sins, but we need to cast them away from our thoughts and desires. Once we turn from the direction of iniquity, we can live in the Spirit.

8.   God is patient and longsuffering (Lamentations 3:22–23). Throughout your daily routines this week, strive to be more like your Heavenly Father in this area, and ask Him to help you be patient with your relationships, inconveniences, deadlines, and even yourself as you grow more in Him. Read Lamentations 3:22–23 and be encouraged.
Responses may vary.

Memory Verses

"It is of the LORD's mercies that we are not consumed, because his compassions fail not. They are new every morning: great is thy faithfulness."—LAMENTATIONS 3:22–23

The Conscientious Mind

Key Verses

ECCLESIASTES 12:13–14

13 *Let us hear the conclusion of the whole matter: Fear God, and keep his commandments: for this is the whole duty of man.*
14 *For God shall bring every work into judgment, with every secret thing, whether it be good, or whether it be evil.*

Lesson Summary

This lesson teaches about the response of those on Mars' Hill to Paul's insistent and convicting plea—they didn't listen! Many people have seared consciences when it comes to hearing the truth of God's Word, and because of their deadened ears to God's plea, they mock, rebel, and turn from repentance. This lesson centers on the study of a seared conscience and the detrimental effects it can have.

Lesson Aim

To help students understand that we only have one life, and this life is the only chance we get to prepare to meet God.

Lesson Goals

At the conclusion of this lesson, students should:

1. Understand the biblical definition of a seared conscience.

2. Understand that we will one day give an account to God.

3. Acknowledge that what we have embraced as truth—God's Word—is going to come under attack.

4. Search their conscience—asking the Holy Spirit to reveal if there is any sin they are holding on to that has become deadened over time.

5. Choose to live with the continual thought that one day they will meet God.

Teaching Outline

I. God's Word Declares an Inescapable Reckoning
  A. Our sure accountability
  B. Our soon appointment

II. God's Word Declares an Incredible Reality
  A. No one is exempt.
  B. No one can escape.

III. God's Word Declares an Impenitent Rebellion
  A. God has revealed clearly.
  B. Man has rejected consciously.

IV. God's Word Declares an Impending Removal
  A. A revealing mercy
  B. A restricted moment

The Conscientious Mind

Text

ACTS 17:31–33

31 Because he hath appointed a day, in the which he will judge the world in righteousness by that man whom he hath ordained; whereof he hath given assurance unto all men, in that he hath raised him from the dead.

32 And when they heard of the resurrection of the dead, some mocked: and others said, We will hear thee again of this matter.

33 So Paul departed from among them.

Introduction

When a change of mind takes place (repentance), the conscience becomes sensitive again. Sin has a deadening effect on our hearts and minds. Paul speaks about this process which takes place over time, *"Now the Spirit speaketh expressly, that in the latter times some shall depart from the faith, giving heed to seducing spirits, and doctrines of devils; Speaking lies in hypocrisy; having their conscience seared with a hot iron"* (1 Timothy 4:1–2).

Illustration

Years ago I had the privilege of witnessing to an old rancher in Montana by the name of Holly Croy. He didn't have much time for me as he thought all preachers were lazy and not worth much. Having been raised on a farm, I decided to try to prove to him that I could work as hard as he could. I arrived the next morning at 5:00 AM to help him brand his cattle. What an experience! For the next ten hours I wrestled with steers in the dirt and manure of that outdoor corral. Mr. Croy branded the old-fashioned way—rope the steers, tackle them to the ground, get the hot irons out of the fire, and apply that red-hot metal to the flank. Those steers would bawl and jerk, and it took every fiber of my body to hold them down. The stench of the burning flesh stayed in my nostrils for weeks afterwards. (By the way, Holly did come to church that week. Years later, two weeks before he died, his wife had the privilege of leading him to Christ.)

When that hot iron is placed on the flank of an animal, it hurts—big time! But once that flesh is "seared" with the hot iron, it is deadened to all feeling. From that point on, that branded area of flesh is crusty and hard. The animal has no feeling in that area. The effects of sin are the same upon our minds. Where we were once sensitive and troubled, we now sense little of the convicting power of God. *"He, that being often reproved hardeneth his neck"* (Proverbs 29:1). *"Who being past feeling have given themselves*

over unto lasciviousness, to work all uncleanness with greediness" (Ephesians 4:19).

But there is hope, *"For the word of God is quick, and powerful, and sharper than any twoedged sword, piercing even to the dividing asunder of soul and spirit, and of the joints and marrow, and is a **discerner of the thoughts and intents of the heart"*** [Emphasis mine] (Hebrews 4:12). And that is exactly why the apostle stands to preach here in the midst of all the pagan altars. He is fully aware that there is but one thing that can break through the hardness of these hearts and bring about a change of mind. No doubt the words of the weeping prophet burned in his heart as he spoke, *"The prophet that hath a dream, let him tell a dream; and he that hath my word, let him speak my word faithfully. What is the chaff to the wheat? saith the LORD. Is not my word like as a fire? saith the LORD; and like a hammer that breaketh the rock in pieces?"* (Jeremiah 23:28–29).

I. God's Word Declares an Inescapable Reckoning

A. *Our sure accountability*

"Because he hath appointed a day, in the which he will judge the world in righteousness by that man whom he hath ordained" (Acts 17:31). When God's Word begins to break through, it sobers us to the fact that we are accountable to God. Daniel Webster was once asked, "What is the greatest thought that can occupy a man's mind?" After a slight hesitation he responded, "The greatest thought that can occupy a man's mind is his accountability to God."

Dr. Bob Jones, Sr. was working in his office one day at Bob Jones College in Cleveland, Tennessee, when a student walked in unannounced. Dr. Jones, sensing

WHAT'S ON YOUR MIND?

that someone had stepped into the room, said without looking up from his work, "May I help you?" The young lady responded, "I just came to tell you that I am going to kill myself." Without taking his eyes off of his work, Dr. Jones said, "I'm sorry, you can't do that." She said, "I'm not kidding, I'm going to commit suicide!" Dr. Jones again responded with, "I'm sorry, you can't." Raising her voice, the young lady said, "Don't make fun of me! I'm tired of living. I'm going to end it all today!" Looking up into her eyes, Dr. Jones said firmly, "I'm sorry, you can't do that. You're going to live somewhere forever."

B. *Our soon appointment*

How true his statement was, for *"...as it is appointed unto men once to die, but after this the judgment"* (Hebrews 9:27). We may be well prepared for life, but are we prepared to die? Our families, our jobs, our social standing, our finances may all be in good order, but God says, *"Prepare to meet thy God"* (Amos 4:12). When you boil it all down, life is nothing more than our opportunity to prepare to meet God! It is **An Inescapable Reckoning.**

> **TEACHING TIP**
>
> *Describe a scene where an employee knows he will check in with his boss at the end of the week. The employee, however, loses concentration and wastes his time surfing the Internet, emailing friends, and putting off projects. Play out how the meeting with his boss will go, and liken this scenario to our lethargic mentality of what our future meeting with God may look like.*

II. God's Word Declares an Incredible Reality

God's Word always gets personal. We don't mind sermons that condemn David, or Peter, or Judas. Secretly, we hope sinners get what they deserve. But when God's finger points at us—that's a different story.

A. No one is exempt.

The Spirit of God now gazes into the eyes of these religious intellectuals on Mars' Hill as Paul declares, *"…whereof he hath given assurance unto all men, in that he hath raised him from the dead"* [Emphasis mine] (Acts 17:31). No one is exempt from this appointment with God. Earthly power will win you no favors. Earthly riches will not bribe you an escape. Your social graces and popularity will be worthless as you stand alone before God! People convince themselves that a loving God would not send anyone to Hell—surely He will allow them past His judgment into Heaven.

Listen to the sobering words of Ezekiel, *"Now is the end come upon thee, and I will send mine anger upon thee, and will judge thee according to thy ways, and will recompense upon thee all thine abominations. And mine eye shall not spare thee, neither will I have pity: but I will recompense thy ways upon thee, and thine abominations shall be in the midst of thee: and ye shall know that I am the LORD"* (Ezekiel 7:3–4). Later in the same chapter he informs us that our money will not bribe God, *"They shall cast their silver in the streets, and their gold shall be removed: their silver and their gold shall not be able to deliver them in the day of the wrath of the LORD: they shall not satisfy their souls, neither fill their bowels: because it is the stumblingblock of their iniquity"* (Ezekiel 7:19).

Illustration

As a kid, I dreaded going to the dentist. (I'm still not really fond of it.) My parents would make me go, and I always had cavities. I inherited soft teeth from my father and no matter how hard I brushed, every visit to the dentist chair became my "electric chair." I can still hear that old rotary drill grinding inside my mouth. Without numbing gel or gas, I can still feel that electric bolt of pain striking the nerve of my jaw and reverberating all the way down to my toes! When I went to college I decided I would never make another dentist appointment in my life! I kept that vow for over ten years and I'm paying dearly for it now. The truth is, avoiding the dentist did not exempt me from the consequences, and no person will be exempt from the judgment of God.

B. No one can escape.

No matter how hard we try, no one will escape this appointment of judgment before God. *"For we must all appear before the judgment seat of Christ; that every one may receive the things done in his body, according to that he hath done, whether it be good or bad"* (2 Corinthians 5:10). Regardless of our status, John declares, *"I saw the dead, small and great, stand before God"* (Revelation 20:12). After 222 verses, Solomon, the wisest man to ever live, summarized it all with, *"Let us hear the conclusion of the whole matter: Fear God, and keep his commandments: for this is the whole duty of man. For God shall bring every work into judgment, with every secret thing, whether it be good, or whether it be evil"* (Ecclesiastes 12:13–14).

The **Incredible Reality** is that no matter who we are or what we have done, whether saved or lost, we will meet God! What if it were today? As the old hymn says, would it be a "glad day"? I'm afraid for many, the words will have to change to "sad day." Take John's admonition, *"And now, little children, abide in him; that, when he shall appear, we may have confidence, and not be ashamed before him at his coming"* (1 John 2:28).

III. God's Word Declares an Impenitent Rebellion

A. God has revealed clearly.

On occasion, in soulwinning, I have met someone who says, "I'm an atheist." I always respond, "God doesn't believe you." (It is fair. They don't believe in God, and He doesn't believe in them.) In all seriousness, there is no such thing as an atheist. *"For the invisible things of him from the creation of the world are clearly seen, being understood by the things that are made, even his eternal power and Godhead; so that they are without excuse"* (Romans 1:20). And according to Romans 2, God has not only revealed Himself to every man, but has written His Word on their hearts and consciences. *"Which shew the work of the law written in their hearts, their conscience also bearing witness, and their thoughts the mean while accusing or else excusing one another"* (Romans 2:15).

B. Man has rejected consciously.

In spite of this inner revelation from God and the preaching of God's Word, there are many who still reject the message. *"And when they heard of the resurrection of the dead, some mocked: and others said, We will hear thee again of this matter"* (Acts 17:32). As Paul pleads with

33

them to change their minds and turn to Christ, they turn away. Have you ever wondered why people reject God? Is it because they do not believe that He exists? Is it because they think the Bible is full of fairy tales and cannot be trusted? No. We have just seen from Romans 1–2 that every man knows there's a God, and His Word has been written on his heart. So why does he reject?

In his second letter, Peter is admonishing Christians to be mindful of the words they have heard before and hold on to them dearly. For he says, *"Knowing this first, that there shall come in the last days scoffers...."* What you have embraced as truth is going to come under attack. There will be those who scoff, ridicule, laugh at and reject this truth. Why? Because they don't believe in God or that His Word is true? No! Read the rest—*"...walking after their own lusts"* (2 Peter 3:3). There's the key. It's not that man does not believe God exists or that the Bible is a hoax; the problem is, he doesn't want to give up his sin! *"And this is the condemnation, that light is come into the world, and men loved darkness rather than light, because their deeds were evil. For every one that doeth evil hateth the light, neither cometh to the light, lest his deeds should be reproved'* (John 3:19–20).

When there is an **Impenitent Rebellion**:

IV. God's Word Declares an Impending Removal

A. A revealing mercy

Be careful how you respond to the conviction of God's Word in your heart. There is a limit to God's grace. Oh, He loves you more than you can imagine and His longsuffering is more than any of us deserve, but there is a limit to His grace. *"The LORD is merciful and gracious, slow to anger, and plenteous in mercy. He will not always chide: neither will he keep his anger for ever"* (Psalm 103:8–9).

B. A restricted moment

While we love verse 8 and rejoice that the Lord is a God of second chances, verse 9 sternly reminds us that our opportunity to respond is limited. God told Noah to build an ark because He was going to destroy the world with water because of the wickedness that had come up before Him. Noah was instructed to preach on sin, righteousness, and judgment to come while he built the ark. But before he ever started, God had set the timetable of His grace, *"And the LORD said, My spirit shall not always strive with man, for that he also is flesh: yet his days shall be an hundred and twenty years"* (Genesis 6:3). Noah would faithfully preach and build. God's spirit would strive with men to repent. And for 120 years men laughed and mocked the message. But when the time had expired, the door was shut by God and it began to rain!

Here on Mars' Hill, Paul faithfully declares God's Word. When that message was rejected, the Bible says, *"So Paul departed from among them"* (Acts 17:33). **Impenitent Rebellion** led to **Impending Removal.** Is God pleading with you today about your sinful life? Is He convicting you about the direction you are going and the way you are living? Thank God for that conviction and don't turn a deaf ear to that still, small voice. He's speaking to you because He loves you and wants to make something of your life.

Illustration

As a sophomore in high school, I had made the varsity football team. One day in practice I got my big break. The starting right guard, though an all-conference player on both sides of the ball, was having an awful practice. He had blocked the wrong player on three consecutive plays, and Coach Friedman, our fiery coach, had seen enough. He ordered Mike Uttech off the field and replaced him with Glenn Griebnow. I laughed as I watched Glenn make his way into that offensive huddle. He never knew what was going on and sure enough, he blocked the same guy Uttech had been blocking. Friedman literally picked him off the ground and threw him to the sideline. With his face bright red and the veins of his neck protruding outward, he marched over to where we scrubs were standing. He yelled, "Give me somebody! Give me anybody that can play that spot!"

I had been looking for a chance to play, and so I raced past him into that offensive huddle. I had memorized all of the blocking assignments in the playbook for all five line positions. There I was, in the huddle with my heroes! Big Frank Boling on one side at center, Cliff Roth the all-conference left tackle on the other side, and Jim Beaver our all-conference quarterback calling the play. As we broke the huddle, I reviewed my assignment in my mind. "Inside; outside; over; closest linebacker." It meant simply that when the ball was snapped, if there was a defensive player in my inside gap, he was mine to block. If there was no one in the inside gap, then I was to block the player in the outside gap. If no one was inside or outside, then I was to block the man over me. If no one was there, I was to block the closest linebacker. As Friedman used to say, "I don't care if the closest linebacker is sitting on the bench—GO BLOCK HIM!"

The ball was snapped, and I nailed the defensive player creating a hole for the running back. The play went for fifteen yards, and I jumped to my feet knowing I had done a great job. But Friedman was already in my face, "WRONG, WRONG, WRONG—GET OUT OF HERE!" I went to the sideline and stood next to Griebnow. Had it not been for my stubborn German pride I would have quit football that night. As I stood there, I felt an arm slip around my shoulder pads. I looked up, and it was big Cliff Roth, the senior left tackle. (Seniors didn't usually put their arms around sophomores!) He said, "John, what's the matter?" I said, "Cliff, you were in there. I blocked the right guy, and you know it. But Friedman climbed all over me." I'll never forget that big farm boy coming around and standing directly in front of me. He grabbed me by my facemask and with a jerk pulled it up next to his. With those beady eyes staring at me, he said, "John, as long as Friedman is yelling at you, he's trying to make you into a good football player. When he stops yelling, go hand in your stuff. He's given up!"

I learned something about football coaches that night and about my Heavenly Father. Oh, I'll be honest, it was humiliating when the coach would yell during those film sessions or throw a clipboard your way during halftime in frustration. But I would smile, because I knew he was still trying to make me into something. I watched the coach stop yelling at some guys and you know what? They never played again. He had given up.

Conclusion

Conviction is no fun, but when God's Word speaks, don't rebel. The worst thing that can happen to you is when that still, small voice goes silent. Listen to the bone-chilling warning of Solomon:

PROVERBS 1:22–33

22 How long, ye simple ones, will ye love simplicity? and the scorners delight in their scorning, and fools hate knowledge?

23 Turn you at my reproof: behold, I will pour out my spirit unto you, I will make known my words unto you.

24 Because I have called, and ye refused; I have stretched out my hand, and no man regarded;

25 But ye have set at nought all my counsel, and would none of my reproof:

26 I also will laugh at your calamity; I will mock when your fear cometh;

27 When your fear cometh as desolation, and your destruction cometh as a whirlwind; when distress and anguish cometh upon you.

28 Then shall they call upon me, but I will not answer; they shall seek me early, but they shall not find me:

29 For that they hated knowledge, and did not choose the fear of the LORD:

30 They would none of my counsel: they despised all my reproof.

31 Therefore shall they eat of the fruit of their own way, and be filled with their own devices.

32 For the turning away of the simple shall slay them, and the prosperity of fools shall destroy them.

33 But whoso hearkeneth unto me shall dwell safely, and shall be quiet from fear of evil.

Study Questions

1. When a hot iron is placed on the flank of an animal, it hurts! But once the flesh has been "seared" with the hot iron, it is deadened to all feeling. Consider this illustration when you read 1 Timothy 4:1–2. What did Paul mean when he said, "...having their conscience seared with a hot iron"?
   Just like flesh is deadened when seared with a hot iron, so is the conscience when it is seared with sin. The conscience becomes deadened to conviction when sin is allowed free reign and rule in the mind.

2. How does the Bible describe someone with a seared conscience? See Proverbs 29:1 and Ephesians 4:19.
   The Bible describes someone with a seared conscience as one who "hardeneth his neck" when being reproved or one who is past feeling anything, therefore giving himself over to sin.

3. Many times, the problem with someone who has a seared conscience is that he does not want to give up his sin. John 3:19 says, "...men loved darkness rather than light, because their deeds were evil." God's Word has the ability to transform you, renew you, and change a seared conscience. Do you have any sin that you are holding onto right now to which your conscience has become deadened over time?
   Answers may vary.

4. Conviction from the Holy Spirit can be uncomfortable, but when God's Word speaks, listen. The worst thing that can happen to you is when that still, small voice goes silent. Be honest with yourself and write briefly

what the Holy Spirit has been convicting you about recently. If you can't think of anything, spend time in prayer asking God's Spirit to convict you of your sins. *Answers may vary.*

5. Daniel Webster once said, "The greatest thought that can occupy a man's mind is his accountability to God." Write out the following verses that correspond with Daniel Webster's statement: Acts 17:31, Hebrews 9:27, and Amos 4:12.
    "Because he hath appointed a day, in the which he will judge the world in righteousness by that man whom he hath ordained; whereof he hath given assurance unto all men, in that he hath raised him from the dead."
    —ACTS 17:31

    "And as it is appointed unto men once to die, but after this the judgment:"—HEBREWS 9:27

    "Therefore thus will I do unto thee, O Israel: and because I will do this unto thee, prepare to meet thy God, O Israel."—AMOS 4:12

6. As Paul pleads with those on Mars' Hill to change their minds and turn to Christ, how do they respond? (See Acts 17:32)
    When Paul pleaded with those on Mars' Hill, some mocked and some said, "We will hear thee again of this matter."

7. No matter who you are or what you have done, whether saved or lost, you will meet God. Referencing 1 John 2:28, describe in your own words what instruction is given to you before this meeting will take place.
    Answers may vary.

8.   What point was the most convicting to you in this study
      and why?
      Answers may vary.

Memory Verses

*"Let us hear the conclusion of the whole matter: Fear God,
and keep his commandments: for this is the whole duty of
man. For God shall bring every work into judgment, with
every secret thing, whether it be good, or whether it be evil."*
—ECCLESIASTES 12:13–14

The Captured Mind

Key Verse

2 CORINTHIANS 10:5

5 *Casting down imaginations, and every high thing that exalteth itself against the knowledge of God, and bringing into captivity every thought to the obedience of Christ;*

Lesson Summary

While some hardened to the message of God from Paul, others heeded. Acts 17 ends on an encouraging note! Just like the few on Mars' Hill who believed God's truth, God wants to capture our minds with truth as well. This lesson focuses on challenging every student to bring *"into captivity every thought to the obedience of Christ"* (2 Corinthians 10:5).

Lesson Aim

To encourage and challenge every student to be spiritually minded—living out every routine, schedule, or situation with the mind of Christ.

Lesson Goals

At the conclusion of this lesson, students should:

1. Desire to have a mind captured by the truth of God's Word.
2. Search their minds for any old truths from God that they have not yet obeyed.

3. Choose to obey the old truths so that God will reveal t them new truths.
4. Cleanse their minds by heeding Psalm 119:9–11.
5. Seek to bring into captivity every thought to th obedience of Christ.

Teaching Outline

I. The Captured Mind Begins with an Openness
   A. A desire to mature
   B. A diligence to meditate

II. The Captured Mind Proceeds with an Obedience
   A. A practice of deference
   B. A problem with disobedience

III. The Captured Mind Culminates in an Ownership
   A. The process of a changed mind
   B. The pertinence of a cleansed mind

The Captured Mind

Text

ACTS 17:34

34 Howbeit certain men clave unto him, and believed: among the which was Dionysius the Areopagite, and a woman named Damaris, and others with them.

Introduction

"Howbeit certain men clave unto him, and believed: among the which was Dionysius the Areopagite, and a woman named Damaris, and others with them" (Acts 17:34). I like the way this chapter ends—on a positive note. While some hardened to the message of God, others heeded. Some mocked, but others melted.

God wants to capture our minds with truth. The world and all of its influences have been in control of our thoughts for too long. It's time to change our minds! It's time to bring *"into captivity every thought to the obedience of Christ"* (2 Corinthians 10:5). *"For to be carnally minded is death; but to be spiritually minded is life and peace"* (Romans 8:6).

I. The Captured Mind Begins with an Openness

A. A desire to mature

When verse 34 speaks of some that *"clave unto him,"* it means that they were open to the truth Paul was preaching. They were hungry and wanted more. What a joy to find people whose prayer is, *"Open thou mine eyes, that I may behold wondrous things out of thy law. I am a stranger in the earth: hide not thy commandments from me"* (Psalm 119:18–19).

B. A diligence to meditate

Is your mind open to God? Just prior to his visit to Mars' Hill, Paul had been with a group of people that he described as *"...more noble than those in Thessalonica, in that they received the word with **all readiness of mind,** and searched the scriptures daily, whether those things were so"* [Emphasis mine] (Acts 17:11).

II. The Captured Mind Proceeds with an Obedience

A. A practice of deference

Not only did these in verse 34 cleave to Paul's words, but they "believed" (Acts 17:34). How precious the Word of

God is when it is received with a desire to obey. *"As an earring of gold, and an ornament of fine gold, so is a wise reprover upon an obedient ear"* (Proverbs 25:12). The blessing of God rests on those who not only hear, but obey. *"But be ye doers of the word, and not hearers only, deceiving your own selves. For if any be a hearer of the word, and not a doer, he is like unto a man beholding his natural face in a glass: For he beholdeth himself, and goeth his way, and straightway forgetteth what manner of man he was. But whoso looketh into the perfect law of liberty, and continueth therein, he being not a forgetful hearer, but a doer of the work, this man shall be blessed in his deed"* (James 1:22–25).

B. A problem with disobedience

Sometimes I hear people say, "God doesn't speak to my heart any more. Must be the preacher isn't doing his job, because God just doesn't speak to me." My friend, the problem is not with the preacher. The problem is, you didn't obey the last time He spoke. God isn't going to show you new truth until you obey the old truth. If I teach my grandkids to ride their bikes on the proper side of the road and they disobey me and ride wherever they

> **TEACHING TIP**
>
> *Pass out a 3x5 card to each member of your class. Take a moment and ask them to think about the last time God spoke to them, have them write it down, and then ask them to write yes if they obeyed and no if they didn't obey God's message. Tangibly seeing a disobedient reaction may have a longer-lasting effect on each class member.*

47

want to, do you think I'm going to let them get behind the wheel of my car? God isn't going to show us the specifics of His Word and His will until we obey Him in the basics.

Have you obeyed the last message you heard? *"Therefore to him that knoweth to do good, and doeth it not, to him it is sin"* (James 4:17).

III. The Captured Mind Culminates in an Ownership

"...Among which was Dionysius the Areopagite, and a woman named Damaris, and others with them" (Acts 17:34). These two converts from the preaching on Mars' Hill did not seem that significant. They are certainly not household names of the faith. What is interesting however, is the last phrase, *"...and others with them."* Dionysius and Damaris **Opened** their minds to the truth, **Obeyed** that truth, and now **Owned** it in such a way as to make an impact on others.

A. *The process of a changed mind*

When a "brainwash" truly takes place, this is exactly what happens. The Word of God changes the mind so the wrong thinking of the past is replaced by right thinking which affects the way that we live. Our minds affect our manners, remember? So if our manners are ever going to change, our minds have to be changed first. When right thinking takes place, right living will follow! Here's the way Joshua of old put it, *"This book of the law shall not depart out of thy mouth; but thou shalt meditate therein day and night, that thou mayest observe to do according to all that is written therein: for then thou shalt make thy*

48

way prosperous, and then thou shalt have good success" (Joshua 1:8). Hearing God's Word causes us to meditate on it; which leads to the doing of it; which produces God's success! God's formula for a changed life starts with a changed mind.

B. The pertinence of a cleansed mind

Does God need to wash your brain out with soap? *"Now ye are clean through the word which I have spoken unto you"* (John 15:3). A lot of so-called "open minds" ought to be closed for cleaning! Your mind is a sacred enclosure into which nothing harmful can enter except by your permission. Why don't you give God permission today to wash it of the wrong thinking of the past and saturate it with the truth of His Word. *"Wherewithal shall a young man cleanse his way? by taking heed thereto according to thy word. With my whole heart have I sought thee: O let me not wander from thy commandments. Thy word have I hid in mine heart, that I might not sin against thee"* (Psalm 119:9–11).

Conclusion

When someone calls you one of those "brainwashed Christians," thank them for the compliment!

49

Study Questions

1. The captured mind begins with what?
   The captured mind begins with an openness.

2. Since we cannot wash our minds out with soap, how can we cleanse our minds? See John 15:3.
   According to John 15:3, we can cleanse our minds through the Word.

3. When right thinking takes place, right living will follow. Referencing Joshua 1:8, summarize the steps to right living and take special note of the first step.
   According to Joshua 1:8, we should meditate on God's Word day and night and observe to do all that is written in the Word.

4. Think back to the last spiritual truth you were taught and then read James 4:17. Have you obeyed that spiritual truth? What does the Bible say about knowing to do good and not doing it?
   Answers may vary.

5. The blessing of God rests on those who not only hear, but who also obey. Write out what the Scriptures say about obedience in James 1:22–25.
   "But be ye doers of the word, and not hearers only, deceiving your own selves. For if any be a hearer of the word, and not a doer, he is like unto a man beholding his natural face in a glass: For he beholdeth himself, and goeth his way, and straightway forgetteth what manner of man he was. But whoso looketh into the perfect law of liberty, and

continueth therein, he being not a forgetful hearer, but
a doer of the work, this man shall be blessed in his deed."
—JAMES 1:22–25

6. In Acts 17:34, the two converts, Dionysius and Damaris, opened their minds to truth in such a way that they had an impact on others. How can you specifically follow God's truth in such a way that you will have an impact on those around you?
    Answers may vary.

7. Because the way you think affects the way you live, wrong thinking of the past needs to be replaced by right thinking. Make a list of two or three thoughts that you struggle with the most (e.g., faithless thoughts, envious thoughts, jealous thoughts, etc.), and list two or three verses that will help you overcome them.
    Answers may vary.

8. An assignment for this week: Every time you hear God's Word expounded upon (whether through preaching or teaching), pray beforehand that God will open your heart and mind to the truth He wants you to hear. Be encouraged as God will answer this prayer and reveal to you the truths and principles He wants applied to your life.
    Responses may vary.

Memory Verse

"Casting down imaginations, and every high thing that exalteth itself against the knowledge of God, and bringing into captivity every thought to the obedience of Christ;"
—2 CORINTHIANS 10:5

The Complacent Mind

Key Verse

MATTHEW 5:6
6 Blessed are they which do hunger and thirst after righteousness: for they shall be filled.

Lesson Summary

Laziness and idleness—these two qualities are far too prevalent in this generation. Students have a hard time doing their homework because they just don't feel like it. Adults are no longer as well-read because they prefer a TV sitcom over a good book. Our generation has become experts at being ignorant; however, the Apostle Paul personally demonstrates how to avoid having a lazy and idle mind. This lesson focuses on how Paul challenged his mind, searched the Scriptures, gave attendance to reading, and developed a sound mind.

Lesson Aim

To develop a sound mind by searching the Scriptures, listening to preaching, and developing good reading habits.

Lesson Goals

At the conclusion of this lesson, students should:

1. Desire to study and search out the Scriptures.
2. Stir and challenge their minds with the preaching of God's Word.

3. Cease from being lazy or idle—giving no chance for th
devil to tempt them.
4. Motivate themselves to be better readers.
5. Understand that one truth from the Bible is worth mor
than all the wisdom of man.

Teaching Outline

I. The Challenge of a Searching Mind
   A. Give attendance to reading.
   B. Give adherence to ruminating.

II. The Challenge of a Stirred Mind
   A. The stirring of exhortation
   B. The seduction of elapsing

III. The Challenge of a Sound Mind
   A. The order for a sound mind
   B. The obedience of a sound mind

The Complacent Mind

Text

1 TIMOTHY 4:13

13 *Till I come, give attendance to reading, to exhortation, to doctrine.*

Introduction

Both the body and the brain have a tendency to be lazy! Modern technology allows and encourages us to put our brains in neutral and let the television, the internet, the video game, or cell phone do the thinking for us. People boast of being broad-minded but are too lazy to think about what is right or wrong.

In Paul's second letter to Timothy, we get some insight into the aged apostle at the close of his life. He isn't sitting in a La-Z-Boy recliner enjoying his Social Security and planning his next trip to Maui. The frail aching body is hunched in the corner of a cold damp Roman prison awaiting execution. He expects at any moment to hear the footsteps of the executioner who will lead him to the chopping block before Nero's throne. He is ready to be offered. These last two letters to young Timothy will enable him to carry the baton faithfully long after Paul is gone. As he shivers in the shadows of that lonely cell, he writes, *"The cloke that I left at Troas with Carpus, when thou comest, bring with thee, and the books, but especially the parchments"* (2 Timothy 4:13). In his dying moments, he desires that the physical, mental, and spiritual all stay right. "My body is cold, so bring me my coat. My mind is weary, so bring me the books. My soul is hungry, so bring me the Scriptures. I have a few more hours to use for Christ. This is no time to be complacent!" What a testimony! Nothing conceals your laurels so much as resting on them.

Paul was practicing what he had preached. Here in 1 Timothy 4, he presents:

I.   The Challenge of a Searching Mind

A. *Give attendance to reading.*

"Till I come, give attendance to reading" (1 Timothy 4:13). Statistics show that Americans spend more money annually on chewing gum than on books. But while reading is important, *what* you read is far more important. The information highway is cluttered with garbage and debris that is detouring many a life from God's destination for them.

I am amazed at how enamored we are with the wisdom of men and how bored we are with God's truth. We're all ears to the talking gurus of ESPN or FOX news, but when our pastor stands to read Scripture, our minds wander and our attitude is, "I've heard all this before." *"For it is written, I will destroy the wisdom of the wise, and will bring to nothing the understanding of the prudent. Where is the wise? where is the scribe? where is the disputer of this world? hath not God made foolish the wisdom of this world?"* (1 Corinthians 1:19–20). No wonder this world is in such a mess. *"My people are destroyed for lack of knowledge: because thou hast rejected knowledge, I will also reject thee, that thou shalt be no priest to me: seeing thou hast forgotten the law of thy God, I will also forget thy children"* (Hosea 4:6).

The following was found written in the fly leaf of Evangelist Billy Sunday's Bible after he died:

> Twenty-nine years ago, with the Holy Spirit as my guide, I entered at the portico of Genesis, walked down the corridor of the Old Testament art galleries, where pictures of Noah, Abraham, Moses, Joseph, Isaac, Jacob, and Daniel hung on the wall. I passed into the music room of Psalms where the Spirit sweeps the keyboard of nature until it seems that every reed and pipe in God's great organ responds to the harp of David, the sweet singer of Israel.
>
> I entered the chamber of Ecclesiastes, where the voice of the preacher is heard, and into the conservatory of Sharon and the Lily of the Valley where sweet spices filled and perfumed my life.
>
> I entered the business office of Proverbs and on into the observatory of the prophets where I saw telescopes of various sizes pointing to far off events, concentrating on the bright and morning star which was to rise above the moonlit hills of Judea for our salvation and redemption.
>
> I entered the audience room of the King of Kings, catching a vision written by Matthew, Mark,

Luke, and John. Thence into the correspondence room with Paul, Peter, James, and John writing the Epistles.

I stepped into the throne room of Revelation where tower the glittering peaks, where sits the King of Kings upon His throne of glory with the healing of the nations in His hand, and I cried out...

All hail the power of Jesus name!
Let angels' prostrate fall;
Bring forth the royal diadem
And crown Him Lord of all.

(W.A. Criswell, *Why I Preach the Bible is Literally True*, Broadman Press, 1969)

I wonder: does that describe your Bible reading this morning? Or did you just check off a box on a Bible reading schedule?

TEACHING TIP

Gather one newspaper clipping, one magazine clipping, one page from a novel, and one excerpt from the Bible. Compare and contrast the information on these pages and show your class how the truth from the Bible will supersede and equip you for life more than any other reading material available.

B. Give adherence to ruminating.

God commands us to *"Study to shew thyself approved unto God, a workman that needeth not to be ashamed, rightly dividing the word of truth"* (2 Timothy 2:15). Jesus said, *"Search the scriptures; for in them ye think ye have eternal life: and they are they which testify of me"* (John 5:39). The ___ 4

gems of Scripture are not all found on the surface. They

must be mined by a diligent search. *"My son, if thou wilt receive my words, and hide my commandments with thee; So that thou incline thine ear unto wisdom, and apply thine heart to understanding; Yea, if thou criest after knowledge, and liftest up thy voice for understanding; If thou seekest her as silver, and searchest for her as for hid treasures; Then shalt thou understand the fear of the LORD, and find the knowledge of God"* (Proverbs 2:1–5).

II. The Challenge of a Stirred Mind

A. The stirring of exhortation

"Till I come, give attendance to…exhortation" (1 Timothy 4:13). The faithful preaching and teaching of God's Word is designed to stir our minds. The Apostle Peter wrote his second Epistle for this very purpose, *"This second epistle, beloved, I now write unto you; in both* **which I stir up your pure minds** *by way of remembrance"* [Emphasis mine] (2 Peter 3:1). Peter's audience had heard the truth many times before, but it was his desire to keep preaching it so that their minds would be established in ~~6~~ truth. *"Wherefore I will not be negligent to put you always in remembrance of these things, though ye know them, and be established in the present truth. Yea, I think it meet, as long as I am in this tabernacle, to stir you up by putting you in remembrance"* (2 Peter 1:12–13).

B. The seduction of elapsing

Today people think they have "killed the fatted calf" if they go to church on Sunday morning. In the Book of

Acts, the people went every day. Maybe that's why the early church was seeing constant revival and we are not *"Not forsaking the assembling of ourselves together, as the manner of some is; but exhorting one another: and so much the more, as ye see the day approaching"* (Hebrews 10:25) Jeremiah said, *"My people have committed two evils; they have forsaken me the fountain of living waters, and hewed them out cisterns, broken cisterns, that can hold no water"* (Jeremiah 2:13). The parking lots of stadiums, movie houses, bars, and shopping malls are packed daily as we fill our lives with all that the well of the world has to offer while there are pews at the front of the church that have not been sat on in years. No wonder our minds resemble cesspools rather than fountains of truth.

You say, "I don't like preaching; it makes me uncomfortable." It's supposed to! It is designed by God to stir up our minds. God's Word comforts the distressed but also distresses the comfortable. *"Take heed, brethren, lest there be in any of you an evil heart of unbelief, in departing from the living God. But exhort one another daily, while it is called To day; lest any of you be hardened through the deceitfulness of sin"* (Hebrews 3:12–13). In a world that daily numbs our minds into believing a lie, we need the exhortation of God's Word to stir us up to truth.

III. The Challenge of a Sound Mind

A. The order of a sound mind

"Till I come, give attendance to...doctrine" (1 Timothy 4:13). Paul exhorted Timothy *"to stir up the gift...which is in thee"* and then in the next verse reminded him, *"For God hath not given us the spirit of fear: but of power, and of love, and of **a sound mind**"* [Emphasis mine] (2 Timothy 1:6–7).

A mind that **Searches** the Scriptures and is constantly **Stirred** up through the preaching of those Scriptures, will be a **Sound** mind.

B. The obedience of a sound mind

People go through life seeking peace and contentment. They try all that the devil has to offer, but nothing satisfies. From party to party and weekend to weekend they are left empty with a craving for more of that which never satisfies. *"The wicked are like the troubled sea, when it cannot rest, whose waters cast up mire and dirt. There is no peace, saith my God, to the wicked"* (Isaiah 57:20–21). Above the din of the world, Jesus calls, *"Come unto me, all ye that labour and are heavy laden, and I will give you rest. Take my yoke upon you, and **learn of me**; for I am meek and lowly in heart: and ye shall find rest unto your souls. For my yoke is easy, and my burden is light"* [Emphasis mine] (Matthew 11:28–30). *"Thou wilt keep him in perfect peace, **whose mind is stayed** on thee: because he trusteth in thee. Trust ye in the LORD for ever: for in the LORD JEHOVAH is everlasting strength"* [Emphasis mine] (Isaiah 26:3–4).

Conclusion

Don't let your mind become complacent. *"Blessed are they which do hunger and thirst after righteousness: for they shall be filled"* (Matthew 5:6). Job said, *"Neither have I gone back from the commandment of his lips; I have esteemed the words of his mouth more than my necessary food"* (Job 23:12). Have *you* eaten today?

Study Questions

1. First Timothy 4:13 says to give attendance to what three things?
   According to 1 Timothy 4:13, we are to give attendance to reading, exhortation, and doctrine.

2. What two evils did the people commit in Jeremiah 2:13?
   The people in Jeremiah 2:13 committed the following evils: they forsook the fountain of living waters, and they hewed them out cisterns.

3. Describe your Bible reading. Is it beneficial, consistent thorough, and applicable to your daily life? After referring to John 5:39 and 2 Timothy 2:15, how can you enhance your time spent in the Bible?
   Answers may vary.

4. In your own words, explain how this statement is true: "A lazy person tempts the devil to tempt him."
   Answers may vary.

5. God's Word comforts the distressed and distresses the comfortable. We need the exhortation of God's Word to stir us up to truth. Write the following verses regarding biblical exhortation: Hebrews 3:12–13.
   "Take heed, brethren, lest there be in any of you an evil heart of unbelief, in departing from the living God. But exhort one another daily, while it is called To day; lest any of you be hardened through the deceitfulness of sin."
   —Hebrews 3:12–13

6. According to Isaiah 26:3, our minds must be stayed upon whom in order to get perfect peace?
Our minds must be stayed in Christ.

7. List the last three books you have read outside of the Bible, and answer the following questions. Were these books edifying? Christ-honoring? Helpful? Or, were they time-wasters? Ineffective? Dishonoring to Christ?
Answers may vary.

8. Be encouraged as you read Matthew 11:28–30. Write out a prayer telling God about the heavy burdens you carry. Choose to lay these at His feet so that He may give you rest.
Answers may vary.

Memory Verse

"Blessed are they which do hunger and thirst after righteousness: for they shall be filled."—MATTHEW 5:6

The Careless Mind

Key Verse

8   *This book of the law shall not depart out of thy mouth; but thou shalt meditate therein day and night, that thou mayest observe to do according to all that is written therein: for then thou shalt make thy way prosperous, and then thou shalt have good success.*

Lesson Summary

Paul went to a lot of trouble to mentor Timothy in the truth of God's Word. The responsibility was now Timothy's. Instead of acting careless with the truths he had been taught, Timothy determined to cultivate truth in his heart so that he could mature spiritually. D.L. Moody once said, "I never saw a useful Christian who was not a student of the Bible." Like Timothy, we can learn to avoid carelessness in our minds by becoming useful Christians—students of God's Word.

Lesson Aim

To discipline our thoughts in the right direction so that we can live the right result.

Lesson Goals

At the conclusion of this lesson, students should:

1. Cultivate the soil of their hearts so that truth can grow and mature to a wonderful harvest.
2. Invest their lives in the ministry of helping others follow Christ.
3. Meditate on Scripture.
4. Consume themselves, like Jeremiah, with a passion to know God's Word.

Teaching Outline

  I. A Cultivation of Truth
- A. A challenge for cultivation
- B. A call for cultivation

  II. A Contemplation of Truth
- A. Apply the Word of God.
- B. Awake to the Word of God.

  III. A Consumption with Truth
- A. A captivating thought
- B. A consuming truth

The Careless Mind

Text

1 TIMOTHY 4:14–15

14 Neglect not the gift that is in thee, which was given thee by prophecy, with the laying on of the hands of the presbytery.
15 Meditate upon these things; give thyself wholly to them; that thy profiting may appear to all.

Introduction

The Danish philosopher, Soren Kierkegaard told the following parable which illustrates what happens when we become careless. "One day a duck was flying with his mates in the springtime northward across Europe. During the flight he came down in a Danish barnyard where there were tame ducks. He enjoyed some of their corn. He stayed for an hour, then for a day, then for a week, then for a month, and finally, because he relished the good fare and the safety of the barnyard, he stayed all summer. One autumn day when the flock of wild ducks were winging their way southward again, they passed over the barnyard, and their mate heard their cries. He was stirred with a strange thrill of joy and delight, and with a great flapping of wings he rose in the air to join his old comrades in their flight.

"But he found that his good fare had made him so soft and heavy that he could rise no higher than the eaves of the barn. So he dropped back again to the barnyard, and said to himself, 'Oh well, my life is safe here and the food is good.' Every spring and autumn when he heard the wild ducks honking, his eyes would gleam for a moment, and he would begin to flap his wings. But finally the day came when the wild ducks flew over him and uttered their cry, but he paid not the slightest attention to them" (Clarence Macartney, *Preaching without Notes*, Abingdon Press, 1937).

Because our minds are capable of receiving, processing, and then storing tons of information each day, a careless attitude toward our thought life is devastating. Here in 1 Timothy, Paul is challenging the life of young Timothy and says, *"Meditate upon these things"* (1 Timothy 4:15). To the Philippians, Paul said, *"Think on these things."* What things? *"Those things, which ye have both learned, and received, and heard, and seen in me…"* (Philippians 4:8–9). The challenge is to discipline our thoughts in the right direction so that we can live the right result. *"I thought on my ways, and turned my feet unto thy testimonies"* [Emphasis mine] (Psalm 119:59). So how do we counteract **A Careless Mind**?

I.   A Cultivation of Truth

A. A challenge for cultivation

"Neglect not the gift that is in thee, which was given thee by prophecy, with the laying on of the hands of the

presbytery" (1 Timothy 4:14). Paul had gone to a lot of trouble to mentor Timothy in the truth of God's Word. The responsibility was now Timothy's. He could neglect what had been sown in his heart and let the thorns of life choke out the Word, or he could cultivate the soil of his heart so that the truth could grow and mature to a wonderful harvest.

B. A call for cultivation

Illustration

There was not a more boring job on the farm than cultivating corn. I enjoyed driving tractors from the time I was a little boy. (They were less complicated and easier to drive in those days.) Like all boys, I love going fast! To get out on the road and do fifteen or twenty miles an hour on a tractor is pretty exhilarating for a little kid! Cultivating corn however, was just the opposite—slow and boring. When the corn was just coming up out of the ground, you had to slowly move through those rows with the cultivator lest you throw dirt on the tiny plants and crush them. But while cultivating corn was tedious, it was extremely important. If weeds were allowed to take over, there would be no crop in October.

Each week your pastor, Sunday school teacher, and perhaps others prepare and then sow truth in your heart through preaching and teaching. Each day as you read the Bible personally, the Holy Spirit guides you into the truth of God's Word. But what are *you* doing with that seed? There are 168 hours in every week. If you spend three hours in church and another seven hours reading your Bible (an hour a day would be extreme for most people), that means you are receiving truth ten hours each week. That means the devil has 158 hours to sow weeds! I think we'd better do some cultivating or the truth is going to die.

The prophets of the Old Testament understood the need to cultivate the heart. Jeremiah cried, *"Break up your fallow ground"* (Jeremiah 4:3). Hosea preached, *"Sow to yourselves in righteousness, reap in mercy; break up your fallow ground: for it is time to seek the LORD, till he come and rain righteousness upon you"* (Hosea 10:12).

It is our responsibility to keep our hearts as "good ground" where the truth can flourish and produce God-honoring results. Don't just "check off" your Bible reading each day and "do church" on Sundays. The Apostle Peter had invested his life in the ministry of helping others follow Christ. Notice his parting words:

2 PETER 3:14–18

14 Wherefore, beloved, seeing that ye look for such things, be diligent that ye may be found of him in peace, without spot, and blameless.

15 And account that the longsuffering of our Lord is salvation; even as our beloved brother Paul also according to the wisdom given unto him hath written unto you;

16 As also in all his epistles, speaking in them of these things; in which are some things hard to be understood, which they that are unlearned and unstable wrest, as they do also the other scriptures, unto their own destruction.

17 Ye therefore, beloved, seeing ye know these things before, beware lest ye also, being led away with the error of the wicked, fall from your own stedfastness.

18 But grow in grace, and in the knowledge of our Lord and Saviour Jesus Christ. To him be glory both now and for ever. Amen.

Growth does not come without **A Cultivation of Truth.**

II. A Contemplation of Truth

A. *Apply the Word of God.*

"Meditate upon these things" (1 Timothy 4:15). Meditation is a lost art. We have too much to *do* to think. Henry Ford said, "Thinking is the hardest work there is, which is probably the reason so few people engage in it." The little prefix "I think" is probably the most over-exaggerated expression of the English language! Amazingly, we spend time thinking about wrong things, but rarely contemplate truth. *"Stand in awe, and sin not: commune with your own heart upon your bed, and be still"* (Psalm 4:4).

Illustration

Growing up on a farm, I learned early in life about the digestive process of cows. A cow can eat an enormous amount of food very quickly. (I would get up every morning before daylight and go out and chop an entire wagon full of alfalfa for them to eat, only to come home from school and have to do it again. In the winter, I would feed each cow a wheelbarrow full of fodder twice a day, which they would devour in about five minutes!) After eating, however, the cow goes through an unusual process. Their food goes down into the first of four stomachs and then is ruminated a little at a time. Contentedly, the cow "chews her cud" for hours as the food is chewed between stomachs.

    While that process in cows is not the most pleasant to ponder, it is this same process that God wants us to have with His Word. *"This book of the law shall not depart out of thy mouth; but **thou shalt meditate therein day and night…**"* [Emphasis mine] (Joshua 1:8). Have you "chewed" on any truth lately?

B. Awake to the Word of God.

If we are going to "chew" on truth all day, it makes sense to get that truth into our lives early in the day. *"O God, thou art my God; early will I seek thee: my soul thirsteth for thee, my flesh longeth for thee in a dry and thirsty land, where no water is"* (Psalm 63:1). Reading and memorizing God's Word early in the day will allow you to "think" on it throughout the day. By the way, the "earlier" a child comes to Christ and is taught to read his Bible the better. Those early truths engrained upon their minds will come back in times of decision and difficulty.

There are many things in life that, when we think about them, bring distress, discouragement, and disaster. A meditation on God's Word will do just the opposite. *"But his delight is in the law of the LORD; and in his law doth he meditate day and night"* (Psalm 1:2). God's Word will direct your thoughts toward the Lord and *"My meditation of him shall be sweet: I will be glad in the LORD"* (Psalm 104:34).

TEACHING TIP

Ask your students to identify areas in which they struggle with pessimism. Start the conversation by sharing an example from your own life. But be sure to also share how you overcame that pessimistic spirit. Don't leave the impression that it's okay to remain discouraged.

III. A Consumption with Truth

A. A captivating thought

"...give thyself wholly to them; that thy profiting may appear to all" (1 Timothy 4:15). D.L. Moody said, "I never saw a useful Christian who was not a student of the Bible."

B. A consuming truth

Jeremiah was obviously consumed with God's Word, "Thy words were found, and I did eat them; and thy word was unto me the joy and rejoicing of mine heart: for I am called by thy name, O Lord God of hosts" (Jeremiah 15:16). The psalmist likewise expresses his joy in God's Word, "And I will delight myself in thy commandments, which I have loved" (Psalm 119:47). "The law of thy mouth is better unto me than thousands of gold and silver" (Psalm 119:72). "O how I love thy law! it is my meditation all the day" (Psalm 119:97). "Thy word is very pure: therefore thy servant loveth it" (Psalm 119:140).

Charles Spurgeon once said, "You should spend so much time in the Bible that your language becomes Bibline." I don't think *Bibline* is a word, but I believe I know what he means. It wouldn't hurt for a "thee" and a "thou" to slip out once in awhile. It would be better than what often slips out!

Conclusion

Izaak Walton said of his Bible, "Every hour I read you, kills a sin, or lets a virtue in to fight against it." Don't let your mind become **A Complacent Mind** or **A Careless Mind**. Fill it with the Truth! Because if you don't, you will be dealing with a big problem. Next week's lesson will tell us just how big.

Study Questions

1. Philippians 4:8 tells us to think on which things?
   Philippians 4:8 tells us to think on things that are true, honest, just, pure, lovely, and of good report.

2. Reading and memorizing God's Word early in the day will allow you to "think" on it throughout the day. List two Scriptures that support this truth.
   Answers may vary.

3. D.L. Moody said, "I never saw a useful Christian who was not a student of the Bible." Do you consider yourself a student of the Bible? Explain your answer.
   Answers may vary.

4. You are to discipline your thoughts in the right direction so that you can live the right way. Psalm 119:59 says, *"I thought on my ways, and turned my feet unto thy testimonies."* Think on your ways, and determine whether you need to turn back to God's Word. What changes do you need to make?
   Answers may vary.

5. The prophets of the Old Testament understood the need to cultivate the heart. Write out their exhortations in Jeremiah 4:3 and Hosea 10:12.
   "For thus saith the LORD to the men of Judah and Jerusalem, Break up your fallow ground, and sow not among thorns."—JEREMIAH 4:3

   "Sow to yourselves in righteousness, reap in mercy; break up your fallow ground: for it is time to seek the LORD, till he come and rain righteousness upon you."—HOSEA 10:12

6. In your own words, describe what it means to delight in the Law of the Lord (Psalm 1:2).
    Answers may vary.

7. What command is given in 2 Peter 3:18, and what steps can you take toward fulfilling it?
    Second Peter 3:18 commands us to grow in grace and in the knowledge of the Lord Jesus Christ. Answers may vary.

8. Using Psalm 4:4 as a guide, spend some quiet time with the Lord, commune with Him, and ask Him to help you cultivate truth in your heart.
    Responses may vary.

Memory Verse

"This book of the law shall not depart out of thy mouth; but thou shalt meditate therein day and night, that thou mayest observe to do according to all that is written therein: for then thou shalt make thy way prosperous, and then thou shalt have good success."—JOSHUA 1:8

The Contaminated Mind

Key Verse

PROVERBS 12:5

5   *The thoughts of the righteous are right: but the counsels of the wicked are deceit.*

Lesson Summary

Unlike light switches, our minds do not turn on and off instantly. Although that would be convenient, it's just not possible. Instead, we have to work on turning our minds off and keeping them closed to wrong influences. Paul was aware of this, and in 1 Timothy 4:16, he warns Timothy to take heed and be careful lest his mind be contaminated. We too can slip into the role of Paul's pupil and learn how to guard our minds from contamination.

Lesson Aim

To guard our minds from wrong influences by keeping our lives pure before God.

Lesson Goals

At the conclusion of this lesson, students should:

1. Seek to rid themselves of any sin in order to keep their vessel clean before God.
2. Not contaminate their minds by false teachers.

3. Saturate their minds with the truth of God's Word.
4. Value God's Word and believe His values.
5. Watch what they say by first watching what they think.

Teaching Outline

I. A Closed Brain-Door Will Keep Your Vessel Clean
    A.   The rule of a clear caution
    B.   The requirement of a clean conduit

II. A Closed Brain-Door Will Keep Your Values Centered
    A.   The content of doctrine
    B.   The concern of deception

III. A Closed Brain-Door Will Keep Your Voice Clear
    A.   A pure mind
    B.   A pleased Master

The Contaminated Mind

Text

1 TIMOTHY 4:16

16 Take heed unto thyself, and unto the doctrine; continue in them: for in doing this thou shalt both save thyself, and them that hear thee.

Introduction

Paul now warns Timothy, *"Take heed unto thyself, and unto the doctrine; continue in them: for in doing this thou shalt both save thyself, and them that hear thee"* (1 Timothy 4:16). **A Complacent Mind** and **A Careless Mind** will lead to **A Contaminated Mind**. Therefore, "take heed!" Keep the brain-door closed to the wrong influences.

I. A Closed Brain-Door Will Keep Your Vessel Clean

A. The rule of a clear caution

"*Take heed unto thyself...*" (1 Timothy 4:16). God commands us to take the water of life to this world. That water, however, needs to flow through a clean conduit. Unfortunately, you cannot separate the message from the messenger. The right content and the right conduit are equally important.

B. The requirement of a clean conduit

Have you ever drunk water out of a garden hose? I remember vividly the first time I did so. What a horrible taste and smell! Now there's nothing wrong with the water. You could go over to that outside faucet and fill a glass with water and not think anything of it. But there's something that changes drastically when that water flows through that old garden hose.

There is nothing wrong with the truth that God has given to us. The water of life is exactly what every person in this world needs. The problem is, God has chosen that it flow through us. That's going to require a clean conduit. "*...Let every one that nameth the name of Christ depart from iniquity. But in a great house there are not only vessels of gold and of silver, but also of wood and of earth; and some to honour, and some to dishonour. If a man therefore purge himself from these, he shall be a vessel unto honour, sanctified, and meet for the master's use, and prepared unto every good work*" (2 Timothy 2:19–21).

Illustration

My family and I have enjoyed owning a few dogs over the years. While we always tried to take good care of them and provide good food and fresh water, I was never once tempted to eat or drink out of the dog's dish! The dog's dish was a nice one—two compartments; sky blue in color; we probably paid all of $2.95 for it at Wal-Mart—but no matter how thirsty I was, never once did I ever get down on my hands and knees and start drinking. I'm sure you understand. While the dog's dish is a vessel, it is a dishonorable one, and no one in his right mind would take in even clean water from such a source. And no one wants truth coming from an error-filled life either. Keeping our thoughts right will keep our vessel clean.

TEACHING TIP

Consider bringing in a clean glass and a dog's dish to illustrate this point visually.

II. A Closed Brain-Door Will Keep Your Values Centered

A. The content of doctrine

"*Take heed…unto the doctrine*" (1 Timothy 4:16). Interestingly, Paul first addresses the conduit, but now stresses the content. It's not only sin that can ruin our thinking, but also the false teachings that constantly swirl around us. By keeping your mind in the Word of God, you will be able to ferret out those things that are contrary to truth. Solomon put it succinctly in the proverb, "*The thoughts of the righteous are right: but the counsels of the*

wicked are deceit" (Proverbs 12:5). You won't fall to the counsels of deceit if your thoughts are right.

B. The concern of deception

 Now be careful, because the Bible teaches us that our own hearts are deceitful. *"The heart is deceitful above all things, and desperately wicked: who can know it"* (Jeremiah 17:9). Because we can't trust ourselves to think right, we must saturate ourselves with the truth that God has given us. *"But strong meat belongeth to them that are of full age, even those who by reason of use have their senses exercised to discern both good and evil"* (Hebrews 5:14). That's why God gave it to us. *"Whereby are given unto us exceeding great and precious promises: that by these ye might be partakers of the divine nature, having escaped the corruption that is in the world through lust"* (2 Peter 1:4).

> **TEACHING TIP**
>
> *Discuss in class how the concept (When God's Word is valuable, your values will be right) is interwoven in the psalmist's life as shown in Psalm 119:97–106.*

When God's Word is *valuable*, your *values* will be right. Notice how those two concepts were interwoven in the psalmist's life:

PSALM 119:97–106

97   *O how love I thy law! it is my meditation all the day.*
98   *Thou through thy commandments hast made me wiser than mine enemies: for they are ever with me.*
99   *I have more understanding than all my teachers: for thy testimonies are my meditation.*

100   I understand more than the ancients, because I keep thy precepts.
101   I have refrained my feet from every evil way, that I might keep thy word.
102   I have not departed from thy judgments: for thou hast taught me.
103   How sweet are thy words unto my taste! yea, sweeter than honey to my mouth!
104   Through thy precepts I get understanding: therefore I hate every false way.
105   Thy word is a lamp unto my feet, and a light unto my path.
106   I have sworn, and I will perform it, that I will keep thy righteous judgments.

III. A Closed Brain-Door Will Keep Your Voice Clear

A. A pure mind

"…for in doing this thou shalt both save thyself, and them that hear thee" (1 Timothy 4:16). When you are thinking purely, you never have to worry about speaking dirty. The old computer saying, "Garbage in—Garbage out" is also true of the mind. "Either make the tree good, and his fruit good; or else make the tree corrupt, and his fruit corrupt: for the tree is known by his fruit. O generation of vipers, how can ye, being evil, speak good things? for out of the abundance of the heart the mouth speaketh. A good man out of the good treasure of the heart bringeth forth good things: and an evil man out of the evil treasure bringeth forth evil things" (Matthew 12:33–35).

83

B. A pleased Master

It was said of Jesus, *"Never man spake like this man"* (John 7:46). Why was this said? Because *"...in him is no sin"* (1 John 3:5). All of us have said things that we regret. Perhaps in frustration you have said, "Why did I say that?" But way before we stop our tongues, we must stop our thoughts. It works the other way too. When we are thinking right, the right words will come when we need them. Have you ever been witnessing to someone and later were amazed that you thought of certain verses to use? God allowed you to speak what you had stored!

Conclusion

Keep the brain-door closed so as to prevent **A Complacent Mind, A Careless Mind,** and **A Contaminated Mind**. In the early verses of 1 Timothy 4, Paul is very specific about why it is so important to keep **A Closed Mind**. With ten-thousand thoughts going through our brain waves every day, it's very easy for the wrong things to slip in.

Study Questions

1. What are the three benefits of having a closed brain-door?
   The three benefits to having a closed brain-door are that it will keep your vessel clean, your values centered, and your voice clear.

2. God has chosen that His Word should flow through you, and He requires that it flow through a clean conduit. What steps can you take in your life to make yourself a clean conduit for God's truth?
   Answers will vary.

3. According to Jeremiah 17:9, can we trust the thoughts in our hearts?
   According to Jeremiah 17:9, we cannot trust the thoughts in our hearts.

4. When God's Word is valuable to you, your values will be right. Refer to Psalm 119:97–106 and explain how this concept directed the psalmist's life.
   Because the psalmist valued God's Word, the values of wisdom, understanding, purity, and loyalty became his foundation, and God's Word lightened his path for living.

5. All of us have said things that we regret. Perhaps in frustration you have said, "Why did I say that?" But way before we stop our tongue, we must stop our thoughts. Write out Matthew 12:33–35 to help you think before you speak.
   "Either make the tree good, and his fruit good; or else make the tree corrupt, and his fruit corrupt: for the tree is known by his fruit. O generation of vipers, how can ye,

being evil, speak good things? for out of the abundance of the heart the mouth speaketh. A good man out of the good treasure of the heart bringeth forth good things: and an evil man out of the evil treasure bringeth forth evil things."—MATTHEW 12:33–35

6. Because we can't trust ourselves to think right, we must saturate ourselves with the truth that God has given to us. List three ways you can saturate yourself with the truth of God's Word.
Answers may vary.

7. There is an old computer saying that says, "Garbage in—Garbage out." As you consider the thoughts you struggle with most, ask yourself, "What 'Garbage in' is filtering into my heart and mind causing me to think these thoughts?" Next, read Matthew 12:33–35, and write out the truths found in these verses.
Whatever is put into the heart will show forth through the tongue. An evil man cannot be a speaker of good things, and a good man will not be a speaker of evil.

8. When you are thinking right, with the Holy Spirit's help the right words will come when you need them. Assignment for this week: Look for a chance to tell someone about the Lord, and allow God to show you that He will give you the right words to say if you first commit your thoughts to Him.
Responses may vary.

Memory Verse

"The thoughts of the righteous are right: but the counsels of the wicked are deceit."—PROVERBS 12:5

The Closed Mind

Key Verse

1 PETER 5:8

8   Be sober, be vigilant; because your adversary the devil, as a roaring lion, walketh about, seeking whom he may devour:

Lesson Summary

In 1 Timothy 4, Paul is very specific about why it is so important to keep a closed mind. With approximately ten thousand thoughts going through our brain waves every day, it is easy for the wrong things to slip in. This lesson focuses on why having a closed mind is essential to living a Christ-pleasing life.

Lesson Aim

To close our minds to unrighteous thoughts as they come through various diversions, demands, and deceptions.

Lesson Goals

At the conclusion of this lesson, students should:

1.   Be aware of Satan's deceptive attacks on God's people.
2.   Realize that God's leading will never contradict His Word.

3. Close their minds to any teaching that makes demands not found in the Bible.
4. Be diligent in their growth toward godliness.
5. Understand that their testimony may affect whether or not someone spends eternity in Heaven.

NOT TRUE

Teaching Outline

I. A Closed Mind Guards against Heretical Deception
   A. The warfare of Satan
   B. The weapon of Satan

II. A Closed Mind Guards against Hypocritical Demands
   A. The tendency to negate biblical principles
   B. The time to nurture biblical principles

III. A Closed Mind Guards against Hopeless Diversions
   A. Guarding our minds from endless diversions
   B. Growing our minds for eternity's destination

IV. A Closed Mind Guards against Hindered Diligence
   A. God's exercise program
   B. God's emphasis proclaimed

V. A Closed Mind Guards against Harmful Departure
   A. Your establishment of faithfulness
   B. Your effect on the future

The Closed Mind

Text

1 TIMOTHY 4:1–8

1   Now the Spirit speaketh expressly, that in the latter times some shall depart from the faith, giving heed to seducing spirits, and doctrines of devils;

2   Speaking lies in hypocrisy; having their conscience seared with a hot iron;

3   Forbidding to marry, and commanding to abstain from meats, which God hath created to be received with thanksgiving of them which believe and know the truth.

4   For every creature of God is good, and nothing to be refused, if it be received with thanksgiving:

5   For it is sanctified by the word of God and prayer.

6   If thou put the brethren in remembrance of these things, thou shalt be a good minister of Jesus Christ, nourished up in the words of faith and of good doctrine, whereunto thou hast attained.

7   But refuse profane and old wives' fables, and exercise thyself rather unto godliness.

8   For bodily exercise profiteth little: but godliness is profitable unto all things, having promise of the life that now is, and of that which is to come.

I.   A Closed Mind Guards against Heretical Deception

A.   The warfare of Satan

"Now the Spirit speaketh expressly, that in the latter times some shall depart from the faith, giving heed to seducing spirits, and the doctrines of devils" (1 Timothy 4:1). The devil never stops attacking. He is on a mission that will not end until he is cast into the Lake of Fire for eternity. *"But evil men and seducers shall wax worse and worse, deceiving, and being deceived. But continue thou in the things which thou hast learned and hast been assured of, knowing of whom thou hast learned them"* (2 Timothy 3:13–14).

B.   The weapon of Satan

The devil has an arsenal full of weapons. He will use accusation. John wrote, *"And I heard a loud voice saying in heaven, Now is come salvation, and strength, and the kingdom of our God, and the power of his Christ: for the accuser of our brethren is cast down, which accused them before our God day and night"* (Revelation 12:10). He will use opposition. That's why Peter said, *"Be sober, be vigilant; because your adversary the devil, as a roaring lion, walketh about, seeking whom he may devour"* (1 Peter 5:8). He will use imitation. He tried that with Jesus when he said, *"All these things will I give thee, if thou wilt fall down and worship me"* (Matthew 4:9).

But no doubt, Satan's number one weapon is deception. *"And the great dragon was cast out, that old serpent, called the Devil, and Satan, which deceiveth the whole world"* (Revelation 12:9). The devil loves deceiving people about immorality, drugs, and alcohol. He has even deceived people about death, as many people think if they commit suicide "they will end it all." But he saves his most sophisticated deception for the spiritual. How many people around the world are deceived about eternal life? What they believe sounds so right. How could something that my church teaches, or that my parents taught me, or that so many people believe, possibly be wrong? *"For such are false apostles, deceitful workers, transforming themselves into the apostles of Christ. And no marvel; for Satan himself is transformed into an angel of light. Therefore it is no great thing if his ministers also be transformed as the ministers of righteousness; whose end shall be according to their works"* (2 Corinthians 11:13–15). The devil's best work is done by those who claim to know God.

Illustration

Years ago in a revival meeting, a young couple that had been newly saved informed their pastor that the Jehovah Witnesses were coming by their home for Bible studies every week. They had not asked them to come; they just showed up, and the young couple didn't want to tell someone who was so "religious" that they weren't welcome. The pastor was very upset that this was happening to these new converts but really didn't know what to tell them. I asked when they normally came, and they told me it was the same time each week. I said, "Well, why don't you invite the pastor and me to come over about that time?"

They were more than happy to have us come, and so we arrived about fifteen minutes before the regular time. Sure enough, they knocked on the door, and the young couple immediately invited them in and introduced them to us. (Of course, we did not reveal we were Baptist preachers.) They started their usual Bible study, and we all listened intently. The young couple kept glancing at us as if to say, "See, this is good—it's all about the Bible."

After about an hour, I was getting weary of their deception and so asked the man, "Do you believe that Jesus Christ was the Son of God and that the only way to Heaven is through Him?" He said, "No," and then tried to explain. As soon as he said "no," the young Christian jumped to his feet and said, "What! You don't believe that Jesus was God! What are you going to teach me if you don't even believe in my Saviour? I'm sorry, you're going to have to leave NOW!"

It's fun to expose error with truth, and that is exactly what the Apostle John instructed us to do.

1 JOHN 4:1–6

1   Beloved, believe not every spirit, but try the spirits whether they are of God: because many false prophets are gone out into the world.

2   Hereby know ye the Spirit of God: Every spirit that confesseth that Jesus Christ is come in the flesh is of God:

3   And every spirit that confesseth not that Jesus Christ is come in the flesh is not of God: and this is that spirit of antichrist, whereof ye have heard that it should come; and even now already is it in the world.

4   Ye are of God, little children, and have overcome them: because greater is he that is in you, than he that is in the world.

5   *They are of the world: therefore speak they of the world, and the world heareth them.*
6   *We are of God: he that knoweth God heareth us; he that is not of God heareth not us. Hereby know we the spirit of truth, and the spirit of error.*

II. A Closed Mind Guards against Hypocritical Demands

A. The tendency to negate biblical principles

"Speaking lies in hypocrisy; having their conscience seared with a hot iron; Forbidding to marry, and commanding to abstain from meats..." (1 Timothy 4:2–3). It is amazing what people believe that cannot be backed up by the Book. People will go to great lengths to find a solution for the sin problem, but totally ignore what the Bible says.

There is a man in the Philippines who allows himself to be crucified on a cross every year in order to try to pay for his sins. This man is a lot like Naaman in the Old Testament who was prepared to give ten talents of silver, a thousand pieces of gold, and ten changes of raiment to the man who could heal him of his leprosy. When Elisha's messenger told Naaman to wash in the Jordan, he got mad and stomped out. Thank God for his servants who reasoned with him, *"My father, if the prophet had bid thee do some great thing, wouldest thou not have done it? how much rather then, when he saith to thee, Wash, and be clean? Then went he down, and dipped himself seven times in Jordan, according to the saying of the man of God: and his flesh came again like unto the flesh of a little child, and he was clean"* (2 Kings 5:13–14).

B. The time to nurture biblical principles

People say, "God told me," or "the Holy Spirit spoke to me." Be careful! God isn't going to contradict His Word. The Holy Spirit will never tell you anything that is not in the Holy Scriptures. *"Howbeit when he, the Spirit of truth, is come, he will guide you into all truth: for he shall not speak of himself; but whatsoever he shall hear, that shall he speak: and he will shew you things to come"* (John 16:13).

In his letter to the Corinthians, Paul made sure that his hearers knew that he was not preaching his opinions or ideas. He didn't want their wisdom to be based on his enticing words or excellent speech, but on the very Word of God. He reminds them that the Holy Spirit will always confirm in their hearts what the Bible teaches. *"But God hath revealed them unto us by his Spirit: for the Spirit searcheth all things, yea, the deep things of God. For what man knoweth the things of a man, save the spirit of man which is in him? even so the things of God knoweth no man, but the Spirit of God. Now we have received, not the spirit of the world, but the spirit which is of God; that we might know the things that are freely given to us of God. Which things also we speak, not in the words which man's wisdom teacheth, but which the Holy Ghost teacheth: comparing spiritual things with spiritual"* (1 Corinthians 2:10–13).

TEACHING TIP

Consider using a whiteboard and make a list of any teaching that makes demands not found in the Bible. Ex: Humanism, sorcery, false prophets (preachers), ministers who heal for money, etc. Discuss how the devil can subtly influence you through these "teachings."

We must guard our minds against any teaching that makes demands not found in God's Word. *"Every word of God is pure: he is a shield unto them that put their trust in him. Add thou not unto his words, lest he reprove thee, and thou be found a liar"* (Proverbs 30:5–6). R.A. Torrey said, "God's Word is pure and sure, in spite of the devil, in spite of your fear, in spite of everything."

III. A Closed Mind Guards against Hopeless Diversions

A. Guarding our minds from endless diversions

"But refuse profane and old wives' fables, and exercise thyself rather unto godliness" (1 Timothy 4:7). A good rule is: If it doesn't *edify—eliminate!* *"Neither give heed to fables and endless genealogies, which minister questions, rather than godly edifying which is in faith: so do"* (1 Timothy 1:4). Some people are well-versed in nothingness. Good things can even keep us from the best things. *"All things are lawful unto me, but all things are not expedient: all things are lawful for me, but I will not be brought under the power of any"* (1 Corinthians 6:12).

B. Growing our minds for eternity's destination

Ask yourself as you start a day or a week, "What on my to-do list will make it into eternity?" Destinations are never reached by taking exits. Notice the single-mindedness of Paul, *"And now, behold, I go bound in the spirit unto Jerusalem, not knowing the things that shall befall me there: Save that the Holy Ghost witnesseth in every city, saying that bonds and afflictions abide me. But none of these things move me, neither count I my life dear unto myself, so that I might finish my course with joy, and the ministry, which I have received of the Lord Jesus, to testify the gospel of the grace of God"* (Acts 20:22–24). Too often we have more than "one thing" that is "needful."

IV. A Closed Mind Guards against Hindered Diligence

A. God's exercise program

"...and exercise thyself rather unto godliness. For bodily exercise profiteth little: but godliness is profitable unto all things, having promise of the life that now is, and of that which is to come" (1 Timothy 4:7–8). How's your exercise program? While physical exercise profits for life, spiritual exercise profits for life and eternity.

Illustration

I have been jogging since 1985. Most days I get five miles in and I believe overall it is profitable. In more recent years, I have mixed in some cycling to keep my body fooled! While not a body-builder by any stretch, I endeavor to lift some weights regularly to keep up some level of strength. I have missed exercising some days to be sure over the years due to travel or other circumstances, but I honestly don't remember the last day I missed reading my Bible. I can think of once or twice when I went out for a run *before* I read my Bible and I regretted it all day. I never want my physical exercise to become my god, but I sure want the Bible to be my guide.

B. God's emphasis proclaimed

It is amazing how diligent and disciplined we can be in areas of little importance. We just have to watch the big game, watch the news, go to work, eat lunch, work out, etc., but how diligent are we in godliness? *"And herein do I exercise myself, to have always a conscience void of offence toward God, and toward men"* (Acts 24:16).

V. A Closed Mind Guards against Harmful Departure

A. Your establishment of faithfulness

The apostle shares his heart in the very first verse of this chapter we have studied, *"…in the latter times some shall depart from the faith"* (1 Timothy 4:1). I wonder how many Christians would still be ministering if they had guarded their minds? There are no sadder phrases in Scripture than, *"For Demas hath forsaken me"* (2 Timothy 4:10); *"…thou hast left thy first love"* (Revelation 2:4); or *"For some are already turned aside after Satan"* (1 Timothy 5:15). You depend on God, but can He depend on you? In God's book of remembrance, I think *faithful* and *famous* are the same word.

B. Your effect on the future

It's not just our lives that are on the line here. Sure, we can make our own choices and live with the consequences, but what about others who are watching? In the last verse of this chapter, as Paul reminds Timothy to *"take heed"* and *"continue"* he says, *"…for in doing this thou shalt both save thyself, and them that hear thee"* [Emphasis mine] (1 Timothy 4:16). When we get to Heaven we will probably be surprised at the number of people who are there *because* of us. Think about it: Have you ever prayed for people to be saved? Have you ever given money to missions? Have you ever handed out a Gospel tract? Have you ever witnessed to someone? We don't get to see most of the results of those efforts, but God takes it all and uses it *"precept upon precept; line upon line…here a little, and there a little"* to bring people to Himself (Isaiah 28:10). I dare say that all of us will meet people in Heaven who are there in some way *because* of us.

It's All of God

But will there be anyone in Hell *because* of us? That is a much more sobering question. Sadly, Paul wrote to the church at Rome, *"For the name of God is blasphemed among the Gentiles through you…"* (Romans 2:24). He told the Corinthian church, *"Awake to righteousness, and sin not; for some have not the knowledge of God: I speak this to your shame"* (1 Corinthians 15:34). What a tragedy that we fail to keep the wrong thoughts from our minds and as a result someone else misses Heaven!

Does knowledge make us saved?

— NO —

Conclusion

Illustration

It was a busy summer day on the farm. It was harvest time and hundreds of bales of hay needed to be brought in "Making hay when the sun shines" is a motto well known to the diligent farmer. But just as we headed to the fields, word came that the cows were out!

We pastured our cows across the river on some rented land. Mom had gotten a phone call from some neighbors that our cows were running across their corn fields, and the neighbors were not happy. We abandoned our task of baling hay and drove as fast as we could to the pasture. Being on the other side of the river, we had to drive several miles to get there and when we did, the cows were everywhere and enjoying every minute of this newfound freedom.

Once out of a pasture, cows can get very disoriented. For the next several hours we chased cows! In the midst of it all, I got stung on the top of my head by a bumble bee. My dad was running cows down from seemingly all over the county; my mom was running back home to get ice for my head, and I was bawling my eyes out. I was just a kid, but I'll never forget that day. Yes, I was the one who left the gate open. My dad never spanked me for my negligence. I guess he figured the bee had inflicted enough pain. People were frustrated, cows were injured, milk production was down for the next two days, and part of the harvest was lost all because I didn't close the gate!

Your mind is the gateway to your heart. Will you leave the gate wide open, or will you guard what goes in and out?

Study Questions

1. We must guard our minds against heretical deception. How can we do this according to 1 John 4:1–6?

We can guard our minds against heretical deception if we do the following: Disregard false teachers and spirits, know the Spirit of God, and depend on God who is greater "...than he that is in the world."

2. Good things can keep us from the best things. First Corinthians 6:12 says, *"All things are lawful unto me, but all things are not expedient: all things are lawful for me, but I will not be brought under the power of any."* As you review your priorities in life, do you see any areas where something good takes priority over that which is best?
Answers may vary.

3. Look at your to-do list this week. Make a list of items from your to-do list that will last for eternity. What items can you add to next week's to-do list that will have more of an impact on eternity?
Answers may vary.

4. We must guard our minds against any teaching that makes demands not found in God's Word. In light of this principle, write out Proverbs 30:5–6.
"Every word of God is pure: he is a shield unto them that put their trust in him. Add thou not unto his words, lest he reprove thee, and thou be found a liar."
—PROVERBS 30:5–6

5. Read 1 Timothy 4:1. What will happen in the latter times according to this verse?
    According to 1 Timothy 4:1, people will depart from the faith because of seducing spirits and doctrines of the devil.

6. Relive the story of Naaman in the Old Testament. He had his own way of searching out a cure for leprosy, and when he was confronted with God's way of healing, he at first refused. Do you have any preconceived beliefs about God or His Word that may keep you from obeying what the Bible truly says (2 Kings 5)?
    Answers may vary.

7. It is amazing how diligent and disciplined we can be in the areas of little importance. You may make time to watch the big game, watch the news, go to work, each lunch, work out, etc., but how diligent are you in godliness?
    Answers may vary.

8. Prayerfully, you will meet people in Heaven who are there because of your prayers, giving, or testimony. However, meditate on this sobering question, "Will there be anyone in Hell because of you?"
    Answers may vary.

Memory Verse

"Be sober, be vigilant; because your adversary the devil, as a roaring lion, walketh about, seeking whom he may devour."
—1 PETER 5:8

The Censored Mind

Key Verse

ROMANS 12:2

2 And be not conformed to this world: but be ye transformed by the renewing of your mind, that ye may prove what is that good, and acceptable, and perfect, will of God.

Lesson Summary

In our modern world of technology, we undeniably need the tool of censorship. We need to put restrictions on the television, the internet, other forms of media, and the list can go on. We also need to censor something far more valuable and important—our minds! Through Spirit-filled men, the Word of God, and a hatred for sin, God shows us how to censor our minds in Ephesians 4.

Lesson Aim

To be "wise unto that which is good, and simple concerning evil" (Romans 16:19).

Lesson Goals

At the conclusion of this lesson, students should:

1. Submit to the authority of pastoral leadership.
2. Use God's Word as a measuring stick to determine if they are closer to salvation or glorification.

3. Choose to mature in Christ through diligent study (the Bible.

4. Grieve when they do not dispel the darkness in order t walk as children of light.

Teaching Outline

    I. Through the Gift of Called Men
        A. The church helps build people.
        B. The congregation has been prepared.

    II. Through the Goal of Christ-like Maturity
        A. A mandated service
        B. A measuring stick

    III. Through the Grieving over Corrupted Morality
        A. The presence of darkness
        B. The power of directness

The Censored Mind

Text

EPHESIANS 4:11–18

11 *And he gave some, apostles; and some, prophets; and some, evangelists; and some, pastors and teachers;*

12 *For the perfecting of the saints, for the work of the ministry, for the edifying of the body of Christ:*

13 *Till we all come in the unity of the faith, and of the knowledge of the Son of God, unto a perfect man, unto the measure of the stature of the fulness of Christ:*

14 *That we henceforth be no more children, tossed to and fro, and carried about with every wind of doctrine, by the sleight of men, and cunning craftiness, whereby they lie in wait to deceive;*

15 *But speaking the truth in love, may grow up into him in all things, which is the head, even Christ:*

16 *From whom the whole body fitly joined together and compacted by that which every joint supplieth, according to*

the effectual working in the measure of every part, maketh increase of the body unto the edifying of itself in love.

17 This I say therefore, and testify in the Lord, that ye henceforth walk not as other Gentiles walk, in the vanity of their mind,

18 Having the understanding darkened, being alienated from the life of God through the ignorance that is in them, because of the blindness of their heart:

Introduction

God desires that the Holy Spirit serve as a censor or filter to our minds so that the things of this world are not able to enter. *"And be not conformed to this world: but be ye transformed by the **renewing of your mind**, that ye may prove what is that good, and acceptable, and perfect, will of God"* [Emphasis mine] (Romans 12:2). This continual process of filtering makes it possible for us to be *"wise unto that which is good, and simple concerning evil"* (Romans 16:19). How can we have this censored mind?

> **TEACHING TIP**
>
> *Consider bringing in a water filter, coffee filter, or air filter to demonstrate visually how we need to filter that which goes in to our mind.*

I. Through the Gift of Called Men
A. The church helps build people.

In verse 11, God lists for us the human gifts to the local church. *"And he gave some, apostles; and some, prophets;*

and some, evangelists; and some, pastors and teachers" (Ephesians 4:11). The twelve *apostles* were the first to follow Christ in His ministry and were later designated as such because they were eyewitnesses of His life after the resurrection (see Acts 1:22). This gift is no longer in existence today because the qualification of being an eyewitness is impossible. Likewise, the *prophets* as listed here are no longer needed because the canon of Scripture is complete.

However, the office of the evangelist and pastor/teacher is still very functional and important today in the local church. Those who preach faithfully the truth of God's Word are given to us as a gift from God to help us have censored minds. Just because you have been disappointed by a preacher or two, don't "throw out the baby with the bathwater." There may be some hypocrites in the pulpit just as there are in the pew, but don't let that dissuade you from the truth that comes to you through the preaching of these God-called men.

I have never met anyone who was living a successful Christian life who was not a part of a local church where the Word of God was being preached faithfully. And I'm not sure that I ever will because God *"hath in due times manifested his word through preaching"* (Titus 1:3). God doesn't need us to build the church, but we sure need the church to build our lives. *"For the preaching of the cross is to them that perish foolishness; but unto us which are saved it is the power of God"* (1 Corinthians 1:18). God has called men to preach and commanded us to submit to the authority of that truth. *"Remember them which have the rule over you, who have spoken unto you the word of God: whose faith follow, considering the end of their conversation"* (Hebrews 13:7).

B. The congregation has been prepared.

One day, at the judgment, each preacher will give an account of his faithfulness to preach the truth, and every person who has heard that truth will give an account of his obedience to that Word. *"Obey them that have the rule over you, and submit yourselves: for they watch for your souls, as they that must give account, that they may do it with joy, and not with grief: for that is unprofitable for you"* (Hebrews 13:17). How sad it is that many people today find excuses week after week to miss preaching services in their churches and then wonder why their minds are stained with worldly thoughts. *"Now ye are clean through the word which I have spoken unto you"* (John 15:3).

II. Through the Goal of Christ-like Maturity

Why did God give us these human gifts (the evangelist and pastor/teacher)? Paul answers that:

EPHESIANS 4:12–16

12 *For the perfecting of the saints, for the work of the ministry, for the edifying of the body of Christ:*

13 *Till we all come in the unity of the faith, and of the knowledge of the Son of God, unto a perfect man, unto the measure of the stature of the fulness of Christ:*

14 *That we henceforth be no more children, tossed to and fro, and carried about with every wind of doctrine, by the sleight of men, and cunning craftiness, whereby they lie in wait to deceive;*

15 *But speaking the truth in love, may grow up into him in all things, which is the head, even Christ:*

16 *From whom the whole body fitly joined together and compacted by that which every joint supplieth, according to the effectual working in the measure of every part, maketh increase of the body unto the edifying of itself in love.*

A. A mandated service

God wants us to become like Him. If that is going to take place, we must filter out that which doesn't assist in that goal. *"For whom he did foreknow, he also did predestinate to be conformed to the image of his Son"* (Romans 8:29A). In a very general sense, there are three stages in God's plan for our lives. There is **salvation**, which takes place the moment you put your faith and trust in Jesus Christ. There is **sanctification**, which begins the moment you get saved and doesn't end until **glorification** when we are with the Lord and then are like Him.

Salvation **Glorification**
Sanctification

If you are a child of God, you are today in the stage of **sanctification** somewhere between **salvation** and **glorification**. If we could picture you on a timeline, are you closer to **salvation** or are you closer to **glorification**? Many people take just a few tiny baby steps after they get saved. The distance between them and the world is minimal. Others, because they place their minds under the control of the Spirit of God and His Word, grow by leaps and bounds, placing great difference between them and the world. When they die or Jesus comes, their step into **glorification** will be minimal, for they have already grown to be like Him.

B. A measuring stick

Using God's Word as the measuring stick, are you close to **salvation** or **glorification**? *"As obedient children, no fashioning yourselves according to the former lusts in you ignorance: But as he which hath called you is holy, so be ye holy in all manner of conversation; Because it is written, Be ye holy; for I am holy"* (1 Peter 1:14–16). Let's grow up and act our age! Many have been saved for years and yet still act like "babes in Christ."

No wonder that the world goes on lost in their sin— they see no difference in those who profess to be different If God has changed your *destiny,* then let Him change you *demeanor,* so that others can see Christ in you. *"But ye are a chosen generation, a royal priesthood, an holy nation a peculiar people; that ye should shew forth the praises of him who hath called you out of darkness into his marvelou light: Which in time past were not a people, but are now the people of God: which had not obtained mercy, but now have obtained mercy. Dearly beloved, I beseech you as strangers and pilgrims, abstain from fleshly lusts, which war against the soul; Having your conversation honest among the Gentiles: that, whereas they speak against you as evildoers they may by your good works, which they shall behold glorify God in the day of visitation"* (1 Peter 2:9–12).

III. Through the Grieving over Corrupted Morality

A. The presence of darkness

When light is turned out, darkness prevails. When a person closes his eyes to the truth of God's Word, no ligh can enter his heart. As a result, he is forced to walk in "the vanity of his mind." *"This I say therefore, and testify in the Lord, that ye henceforth walk not as other Gentiles walk, in the vanity of their mind, Having the understanding darkened, being alienated from the life of God through the ignorance that is in them, because of the blindness of their heart"* (Ephesians 4:17–18).

B. The power of directness

Illustration

I was speaking at a Christian school one morning for chapel. After the invitation at the close of the service, a group of five or six teenagers came up onto the platform to ask me a question. I placed my Bible back on the pulpit and began to talk with these young people. As I did, I noticed there was a young man standing at the foot of the stairs leading up to the platform who was also waiting to speak with me. It was obvious that he was a bit perturbed that others had beaten him to me, as he was now showing his impatience by making funny noises of disdain. Finally, after a few moments of answering questions, the teens made their way off the platform and headed to class. The young man waited until they had completely exited the auditorium and then stomped his foot on every stair on his way up to me.

When he arrived at the pulpit, he threw up his hands and said, "Problems, problems, problems!" I thought, what kind of a nut is this? I looked at him and said, "Son, I don't want to hear any problems." He looked at me rather surprised. Preachers are supposed to listen to problems, but quite honestly, I didn't feel like it. Instead, I asked him, "Are you saved?" He said, "Of course, I'm saved!" I said, "Do you read your Bible every day?" Disgustedly, he said, "No." I said, "Was there ever a time in your life when you read the Bible every day?" He thought a moment and said, "Yeah, about two years ago, I read it every day." I looked into his eyes and asked, "When did your problems start?" He paused and his head dropped. When he looked up, there were tears in his eyes, as he said, "About two years ago."

I put my arm around him and said, "I don't know what it is that's bugging you today, but that is your *problem.*" Jesus declared, *"Ye do err, not knowing the scriptures"* (Matthew 22:29A). Life is going to be filled with all kinds of problems when our minds are not being censored on a regular basis by the truth of God's Word.

Conclusion

Are you reading God's Word daily? Are you in church when the doors are open listening to God's Word being preached? How do we expect to "walk as children of light" when we are doing nothing to dispel the darkness? We must be guided by a **Censored Mind**.

Study Questions

1. We are to protect our minds with the help of the authority God has placed over us. According to Hebrews 13:7 and 17, how are we to respond to our authority?
According to Hebrews 13:7, we are to remember those who have the rule over us. According to Hebrews 13:17, we are to obey and submit to those who have the rule over us.

2. According to Titus 1:3, through what does God manifest His Word?
According to Titus 1:3, God manifests His Word through preaching.

3. To have minds that are Christ-like and mature, we must be a student of the gifts God has given to us. The Apostle Paul answers the question, "Why did God give us human gifts?" Read Ephesians 4:12–16 and summarize his answer.
In reference to Paul's answer, God gave us gifts for the perfecting of the saints, for the work of the ministry, and for the edification of the body of Christ. Our gifts are to work collaboratively in the body of Christ for effectual working.

4. In a very general sense, there are three stages in God's plan for our lives. The first stage is salvation, which takes place the moment you put your faith and trust in Jesus Christ. List and describe the other two stages.
The second stage in God's plan for our lives is sanctification which describes where every child of God is. Sanctification means to be set apart, mainly from that which is not of the Lord. The third stage in God's plan for our lives is glorification. Glorification is reached when we are with the Lord and are like Him.

5. Write out Ephesians 4:17–18—a passage of Scripture
    which admonishes us not to walk in vanity o:
    corrupt morality.
    "This I say therefore, and testify in the Lord, that ye
    henceforth walk not as other Gentiles walk, in the vanity
    of their mind, Having the understanding darkened, being
    alienated from the life of God through the ignorance
    that is in them, because of the blindness of their heart:
    *—*EPHESIANS 4:17–18

6. A continual process of censoring our minds will make
    us wise concerning good and simple concerning evil
    (Romans 16:19). In your own words, why do you think i·
    is best to be simple concerning evil?
    Answers may vary.

7. According to Romans 12:2, how can we be transformed?
    According to Romans 12:2, we can be transformed by the
    renewing of our minds.

8. If God has changed your *destiny*, then let Him change
    your *demeanor*, so that others can see Christ in you. What
    changes can you make this week to clearly show others
    that Christ lives in you?
    Answers may vary.

Memory Verse

"And be not conformed to this world: but be ye transformed by
the renewing of your mind, that ye may prove what is that good
and acceptable, and perfect, will of God."—ROMANS 12:2

The Clean Mind

Key Verse

2 CORINTHIANS 5:17

17   Therefore if any man be in Christ, he is a new creature: old things are passed away; behold, all things are become new.

Lesson Summary

When we get saved, we become new creatures in Christ. Although this is an exciting time, we must realize that we do not become perfect creatures in Christ. The struggle with sin and temptation still exists. Ephesians 4:19–20 gives us the process of how we allow sin into our minds even after salvation, and this lesson focuses on what we can do to keep our minds clean from that sin.

Lesson Aim

To help students understand the value and priority of having clean and pure minds before God, and to help them focus on the biblical way of keeping sin out of their minds.

Lesson Goals

At the conclusion of this lesson, students should:

1. Understand that their conscience may have become insensitive to little sins.

2. Reject the corruption of their thoughts by not playing with little sin.
3. Not feel comfortable or justify doing wrong.
4. Decide not to ignore the communication from the Holy Spirit.
5. Grasp the importance of keeping their minds pure and clean.

Teaching Outline

I. An Insensitive Conscience
    A. A seared mind
    B. A sent message

II. An Invited Corruption
    A. The ditch of wrong thinking
    B. The disaster of woeful transgressions

III. An Increased Continuation
    A. Sin destroys continually.
    B. Sin deceives consciously.

IV. An Inflamed Clamoring
    A. The fire of sin
    B. The fuel of sin

V. An Ignored Communication
    A. The warning issued
    B. The warning ignored

The Clean Mind

Text

EPHESIANS 4:19–20

19 Who being past feeling have given themselves over unto lasciviousness, to work all uncleanness with greediness.

20 But ye have not so learned Christ;

Introduction

When we ask Christ into our lives to save us, the Bible declares that *"…if any man be in Christ, he is a new creature: old things are passed away; behold, all things are become new"* (2 Corinthians 5:17). That being true, how does sin creep back into our lives as children of God? We know that we cannot lose our salvation, for Jesus declared, *"And I give unto them eternal life; and they shall never perish, neither shall any man pluck them out of my hand. My Father, which gave them me, is greater than all; and no man is able to pluck them out of my Father's hand"* (John 10:28–29).

Ephesians 4:19–20 gives us the process whereby we allow sin into our minds. Many a mother, after giving her little boy a bath, has said, "Now stay clean!" Mom wants him to be clean for church or some other important function. But little boys are little boys, and dirt has a way of presenting itself. When God cleansed us from sin at salvation, He desires that we stay clean. But sin has a way of presenting itself, and that attack always begins in the mind.

I. An Insensitive Conscience

A. A seared mind

"Who being past feeling…" (Ephesians 4:19A). Watch out when you no longer sense the Spirit of God speaking to you through His Word! Remember what we said earlier about the brand on the flank of the cow? Like many a branded animal, we must not allow our conscience to be *"seared with a hot iron"* (1 Timothy 4:2).

B. A sent message

God had a message for the prophet Jeremiah to deliver to the nation of Israel, *"Declare this in the house of Jacob, and publish it in Judah, saying, Hear now this, O foolish people, and without understanding; which have eyes, and see not; which have ears, and hear not; Fear ye not me? saith the LORD: will ye not tremble at my presence?"* (Jeremiah 5:20–22). By the time we get to Jeremiah 8, this seared conscience led to a sorry condition, *"Were they ashamed when they had committed abomination? nay, they were not at all ashamed, neither could they blush:*

therefore shall they fall among them that fall: in the time of their visitation they shall be cast down, saith the LORD" (Jeremiah 8:12).

Illustration

Dr. Paul Brand was a physician who did much to advance the treatment of leprosy. As he lived among the lepers to study them and treat them, he would regularly take baths in scalding water. His purpose in this was to discover if there were any parts of his body where he might have lost feeling. He knew that if there was any part of his body that had lost sensitivity to the boiling water, it was there that the leprosy had attacked him (Gordon MacDonald, *A Resilient Life*, Nashville: Nelson Books, 2004, p. 17).

So, where has your life become insensitive? Do we still blush at a curse word or immoral scene on television? Are we still appalled by a lie? Does bitterness or pride bother us or has it become our pet sin? Christians today are allowing words, thoughts, music, friends, entertainment, etc., into their lives that would have bothered their conscience a few years ago. Conscience is that thing that hurts when everything else feels good. Cultivate a clear conscience; it may turn out to be the best friend you ever had. The polluting of our minds begins with an **Insensitive Conscience.**

II. An Invited Corruption

A. The ditch of wrong thinking

"...have given themselves over unto lasciviousness" (Ephesians 4:19). Once the conscience is seared, it is easy to plunge forward into wrong thinking. The door into our

minds has been cracked open, and sin just automatically thinks it has been invited inside. It is amazing how you can't just sin a little. Sin never stays little; it always grows. That little sin in our minds can grow until it causes our whole life's direction to change.

B. The disaster of woeful transgressions

Illustration

Recently, I had my first experience with a kidney stone. I went to bed as normal on a Saturday night after driving most of the day to get to a church so that I could preach the services the next morning. About ten minutes into sleep, I was awakened by an intense pain in my abdomen. I tried everything over the next two hours to rid myself of that horrible pain, but nothing worked. After arriving at an emergency room in a strange town, they gave me some morphine and did a CAT scan. Five hours later, I was given the news: You have a kidney stone—textbook symptoms—you should pass it in the next few hours. As the doctor was sending me home, he instructed me to try to "catch" the stone so that they could study it and find out its cause. As he handed me a "strainer," I asked him what I was looking for? He said, "Oh, you won't be impressed—it's about the size of a grain of sand." I had heard that the pain of passing a kidney stone was like having a baby. I thought, "a grain of sand?" I'm about to deliver a world-class midget! How could such a little thing create so much torment?

Like that grain of sand creating such an intense pain, when we open the door of our minds to the thought of sin, we are asking for big problems. No wonder Paul was so emphatic! *"But put ye on the Lord Jesus Christ,*

120

and make not provision for the flesh, to fulfil the lusts thereof" (Romans 13:14). *"Neither give place to the devil"* (Ephesians 4:27). Solomon in his wisdom warned, *"My son, if sinners entice thee, consent thou not"* (Proverbs 1:10). Evangelist Billy Sunday used to say, "If you don't want to sin, stay out of the devil's neighborhood." There is way too much window-shopping at the mall of sin. Only fools fool with sin. Flirting with temptation always leads to romance with sin.

III. An Increased Continuation

A. Sin destroys continually.

"...to work all uncleanness" (Ephesians 4:19C). Like a cancer, sin begins to work its way into every part of our lives. Adam and Eve allowed a *doubt* and ended up in *disobedience.* Lot allowed a *division* and ended up in *drunkenness.* Achan allowed *covetousness* and ended up in a *cemetery.* Samson allowed a *look* and ended up in *lust.* David started out *missing from battle,* and ended up *murdering in brutality.*

"But every man is tempted, when he is drawn away of his own lust, and enticed. Then when lust hath conceived, it bringeth forth sin: and sin, when it is finished, bringeth forth death" (James 1:14–15). No sin starts with murder, or rape, or robbery. It begins with a thought and grows into an action.

B. Sin deceives consciously.

Have you ever gone early to a major league baseball game? After the teams take a couple of hours of batting and infield practice, the field is cleared so that the grounds crew can ready the field for play. Every person on the field over the next few minutes has a job to do—some are watering down the infield while others are putting new bases in place. Usually, one man works alone around home plate. His job is to carefully re-chalk the batter's box. Two boxes are neatly placed on both sides of the plate. To stand outside of these boxes while hitting is illegal, and so they are meticulously measured and chalked.

When "Play Ball!" is heard echoing from the home plate umpire, the first batter steps to the plate. If you watch, his first move is to try to erase the back of the batter's box with his spikes. He deletes that clearly marked line by mixing the chalk with dirt until it is hardly discernible. Now with the line no longer clear, he "cheats" back in the box as far as he can without being called out, so as to see the pitch for as long as possible.

God went to a lot of trouble to give us His clearly defined commandments. How casually we rub them out and rationalize that we are "close" to the "batter's box" of His Word. Edmund Burke writes, "The instances are exceeding rare of man immediately passing over a clear marked line from virtue into declared vice and corruption. There are middle tints and shades between the two extremes; there is something uncertain on the confines of the two empires which they must pass through, and which renders the change easy and imperceptible" (George Sweeting, *Who Said That?*, Chicago: Moody Press, 1994, p. 117).

David never dreamed he would commit murder after such a track record of victory, but the problem with a little sin is that it never stays little.

IV. An Inflamed Clamoring

A. The fire of sin

"...with greediness" (Ephesians 4:19D). The fire of sin is hard to put out! The devil has plenty of fuel to throw on that fire to keep it burning for a long time.

Illustration

When I was a teenager, I took care of a cemetery. There was a lot of brush in the fence line, and so my dad and I spent several days clearing out all of the vines and thorns that had grown into the fence. After several days, we had quite a pile of brush across the road from the cemetery down in a ravine.

A few days later, my dad told me to ride my bike over there and burn that pile of brush. I took some matches and made my way eagerly to the ravine. This was going to be fantastic fire, and I was looking forward to watching the inferno. I lit a couple of small twigs at the bottom of that brush pile, but they would burn for just a few seconds and then go out. I found some old newspaper and tried lighting it, but the same thing happened. Those stumps and branches were just too "green" to burn, so I decided to add some "fuel to the fire."

I walked over to the little storage shed that we had at the cemetery and got a large ten-gallon drum of gasoline. My theory was actually pretty good, but my methods were flawed. I again lit some newspaper and got it burning at the bottom of the pile. I stood back a few feet and took the drum of gasoline and with the lid open, I clumsily slung some gasoline toward the fire. I don't remember much about the next few seconds. An inferno would be an understatement, as the flames shot up not only from the brush pile but from the ten-gallon drum that I was still holding! I threw that drum into the fire and ran. When I heard the explosion of that drum I dove to the ground, covered my head and hoped that none of the shrapnel from that exploding drum would fall on me.

B. The fuel of sin

Allow a little sin into your mind and the devil will be sure to add the fuel to that sin. Within a very short time, you will have a fire of sin burning in your life that will be difficult to extinguish. We can get to the point where we enjoy the sin that we once abhorred. *"Who knowing the judgment of God, that they which commit such things are worthy of death, not only do the same, but have pleasure in them that do them"* (Romans 1:32). Your appetite for sin will increase more and more, *"...the mouth of fools feedeth on foolishness"* (Proverbs 15:14). Sin that was once feared is now commonplace. *"How much more abominable and filthy is man, which drinketh iniquity like water?"* (Job 15:16). Doing wrong is now as normal as getting a drink of water.

This **Insensitive Conscience, Invited Corruption, Increased Continuation,** and **Inflamed Clamoring** is all a result of:

V. An Ignored Communication

A. The warning issued

"But ye have not so learned Christ" (Ephesians 4:20). Paul reminds us that we did not learn this wrong pattern from Christ. All through the process of closing our minds to

God, the Holy Spirit tries to warn us. Are you ignoring God's warnings today? Isaiah 65:12 says, *"…because when I called, ye did not answer; when I spake, ye did not hear; but did evil before mine eyes, and did choose that wherein I delighted not."*

TEACHING TIP

Take a moment in class and share a personal testimony of the last time you heard the Holy Spirit give you a warning. Talk about the importance of heeding that warning immediately.

B. The warning ignored

It's one thing to ignore the counsel of good people in your life, but to turn a deaf ear to God is a very dangerous trend. *"He that hath an ear, let him hear…"* (Revelation 2:29). The saddest places in the Bible are the times when the voice of God is ignored. *"O Jerusalem, Jerusalem, thou that killest the prophets, and stonest them which are sent unto thee, how often would I have gathered thy children together, even as a hen gathereth her chickens under her wings, and ye would not"* (Matthew 23:37).

Illustration

When I first started out in evangelism, my family and I traveled in a Chevy Suburban and pulled a twenty-five foot Airstream trailer. Having grown up on a farm, I never struggled with some of the challenges of pulling that trailer that some of my fellow-evangelists did. But on one particular occasion, my over-confidence got me into trouble.

I was preaching for the Dublin Christian Academy in Dublin, New Hampshire for a school revival. Their academy is located on the top of a New England mountain, and it was December. We got our trailer up there without any problems and enjoyed being on the campus for the various chapels that took place during the day. In the evenings, we would drive down the mountain and over to the town of Peterborough where we would hold revival services for a new church plant at the Town Hall.

As Friday approached, I began to do some planning for our departure. We were scheduled to begin meetings in Pittsburgh on Sunday, and the forecast there in New Hampshire was for freezing temperatures with some rain or snow. Since we would need to leave after the service on Friday night in order to make it to Pittsburgh by Sunday, I decided to hook up the trailer after the last chapel and take it down the mountain before the temperatures dropped below freezing. I knew that winding road down the mountain would get icy as the temperature dropped. The pastor and his family had invited us to eat at their house at five, and so I had planned to drive into town and park the trailer in one of the store parking lots near the Town Hall and walk to the pastor's house.

Everything worked fine as we made it down the mountain and into town without any problems. But as I got to the main street of town, it suddenly dawned on me that it was Friday night during the Christmas season and all of the stores were open until late. Thus, all of the parking lots were full, and there was no place to park our rig. By now it was dark and close to five o'clock, but I knew that I had no choice but to go back out to the highway and circle back over the mountain to the pastor's home. This was the day prior to cell phones, and

I didn't want to be late to the pastor's home. I knew that we were about fifteen minutes away if all went well, but it was nearing five o'clock.

As I drove down the main street, I remembered that there was a one-lane road that went over the mountain and came out about a block from the pastor's house. We had driven it one day as we were out soulwinning. I remembered that it was the road right after the public library. As I approached that corner, I told my family that I knew a shortcut. Immediately, I sensed the Holy Spirit saying, "Don't do it!" I rounded the corner anyway and pressed the accelerator down in order to gain some speed up this incline that was probably about a half mile in distance.

The Holy Spirit kept saying, "Stop! Don't do this! Turn around now!" But I ignored that voice. That 454 Chevy engine was roaring now as we chugged toward the top. About twenty yards from the crest, my rear wheels began to spin on the icy pavement below. (It was colder near the top and the moisture on the road had frozen.) No problem, I thought. I put my foot on the brake and allowed a few seconds to pass, knowing from experience that the heat of my spinning tires would melt the ice beneath them, and we would be able to move forward momentarily. As I took my foot off of the brake and applied the accelerator however, we began to slide backwards. As I hit the brake, the truck and trailer began to jackknife. When I would let off the brake, I could straighten the rig slightly, but as soon as I would hit the brake again we would jackknife and slide a little closer to the edge of that one-lane road.

On the passenger side, where my wife was sitting, there was a deep ravine that plunged about five hundred feet down with a few young pine trees that wouldn't have held a snowmobile on that mountain much less a twenty-thousand pound rig! On my side there was a deep ditch of about fifty feet that didn't look any more inviting. At one point, I decided to set the parking brake and get out and take a look at our situation since it was by now completely dark. As I got out of the truck however, it began to slide past me, so jumping back in I announced to my family, "WE ARE GOING TO DIE!"

We managed to slip and slide backwards down that mountain about a hundred yards when my wife informed me that if we slid any closer to the edge on her side, we were going over. I again made sure that everybody in the truck knew that they were saved, we said our prayers, and I decided to take my foot off of the brake, close my eyes, and hope for the best. Because of our jackknifed position, the trailer pulled our truck off of the road to the left where there "just so happened" to be a driveway that we hit dead center and plunged into a giant bank of snow backwards!

It took awhile to shovel out the back of that trailer from the snow, but we were able to pull out of that driveway and head back down the mountain and to the pastor's house. (We were only about an hour late for dinner, but I wasn't very hungry anyway.) I don't think that still, small voice ever stopped talking until we got to Pittsburgh Saturday night! He just kept saying, "I told you so!" What's that voice telling you today? Don't ignore His communication.

Study Questions

1. When we open the door of our minds to the thought of sin, we are asking for big problems. The following Scriptures contain warnings about sin. Look up these verses and write a sentence summarizing each verse: Romans 13:14, Ephesians 4:27, and Proverbs 1:10.

    Romans 13:14: In order to make no provision for the flesh—giving into wrong desires—we need to put on the Lord Jesus Christ.

    Ephesians 4:27: The devil deserves no place in our lives. Sometimes, we belittle sin, but we still give it a place in our schedule. According to this verse, we ought not give the devil or his temptations any ranking in our lives.

    Proverbs 1:10: Sinners will entice or persuade us to sin. When—not if—this occurs, this verse says to say "no" to them.

2. In the battle of trying to keep our minds clean from sin, the devil tries to create an appetite for sin. What do the following verses say about having an appetite for sin: Proverbs 15:14 and Job 15:16?

    Proverbs 15:14 teaches that the appetite for sin will increase more and more, and Job 15:16 teaches that sin that was once feared is now commonplace.

3. Through the process of closing our minds to God, the Holy Spirit tries to warn us. Are you ignoring God's warnings today? Does Isaiah 65:12 describe your response to God's warnings? Explain your answer.

    Answers may vary.

4. Describe the last time you sensed God's Holy Spirit leading you. What was He asking, and how did you respond?
    Answers may vary.

5. Sin begins with a thought and grows into an action. Write out James 1:14–15—the Bible's clear process of sin.
    "But every man is tempted, when he is drawn away of his own lust, and enticed. Then when lust hath conceived, it bringeth forth sin: and sin, when it is finished, bringeth forth death."—JAMES 1:14–15

6. When you read Romans 1:32, you will find that the appetite for sin only grows. Meaning, we can get to the point where we enjoy the sin that we once detested. Think back to the time when you first became a Christian. God was now living inside of you, and you were determined to live your best for Him. Are there any sinful habits you have let back into your life since you became a Christian?
    Answers may vary.

7. According to 2 Corinthians 5:17, what is to be "passed away"?
    According to 2 Corinthians 5:17, old things are to be passed away.

8. Ephesians 4:20 says, *"But ye have not so learned Christ."* Paul warned that allowing sin into a clean mind is not of Christ. Determine this week to learn Christ—learn His

way of turning from temptation, His way of rebuking sin, and His way of following God's leading.
Responses may vary.

Memory Verse

"Therefore if any man be in Christ, he is a new creature: old things are passed away; behold, all things are become new."
—2 CORINTHIANS 5:17

The Conformed Mind

Key Verse

2 CORINTHIANS 3:5

5   Not that we are sufficient of ourselves to think any thing as of ourselves; but our sufficiency is of God;

Lesson Summary

This lesson introduces an error-proof formula for every Christian who desires to have the mind of Christ. It encourages each Christian to please God in the sincerest way by conforming his thoughts, desires, reactions, opinions, and beliefs in such a way that emulates Christ. These three practical steps of conforming our minds are intended to motivate us to godliness and holiness.

Lesson Aim

To establish a desire in the heart of each Christian to conform his mind to the mind of Christ.

Lesson Goals

At the conclusion of this lesson, students should:

1.   Search their minds and repent of any sinful patterns they find in their lives.
2.   Realize that Satan will tempt them no matter the circumstances.

3. Determine to resist Satan's luring with the power of the Holy Spirit.

4. Choose to implement the replacement theory by putting off sinful habits and putting on a Spirit filled life.

Teaching Outline

I. Repent of Sinful Patterns
   A. The realization of sinful thought patterns
   B. The repentance of sinful thought patterns

II. Resist with Spirit-Filled Power
   A. The enhancement of the Spirit
   B. The emptying of self

III. Replace with Scriptural Precepts
   A. Putting off is equivalent to repentance.
   B. Putting on is equivalent to restoration.

The Conformed Mind

Text

EPHESIANS 4:22–24

22 That ye put off concerning the former conversation the old man, which is corrupt according to the deceitful lusts;
23 And be renewed in the spirit of your mind;
24 And that ye put on the new man, which after God is created in righteousness and true holiness.

Introduction

We are never going to be able to think right on our own. — Q#1
"Not that we are sufficient of ourselves to think any thing as of ourselves; but our sufficiency is of God" (2 Corinthians 3:5).
Our minds must be conformed to God's mind if we are going .— Q#2
to please Him. That has been God's desire since the day He
saved us, *"For whom he did foreknow, he also did predestinate to be conformed to the image of his Son…"* (Romans 8:29).

135

In these next few verses of Ephesians 4, Paul gives us three practical steps to take if we are going to have minds that are conformed to Christ.

I. Repent of Sinful Patterns

A. The realization of sinful thought patterns

"That ye put off concerning the former conversation the old man, which is corrupt according to the deceitful lusts" (Ephesians 4:22). Put off! Get rid of! Repent! Change your mind! "Repent therefore of this thy wickedness, and pray God, if perhaps the **thought of thine heart** may be forgiven thee" [Emphasis mine] (Acts 8:22).

Have you ever noticed that we have a certain pattern of thought? It seems that some thoughts, no matter how hard we try to ignore them, continue to return. Sometimes these thoughts are resurrected from our lives before we were saved. Notice Paul speaks of the "former conversation" or the "unsaved mind." He also tells us to rid our minds of that which is "corrupt" in this verse. That would speak of the "unholy mind"—those things that we have allowed in as sinful thought patterns. Then he says we must turn from "deceitful lusts" which speak of the thoughts that have been entertained by an "unbridled mind." The unsaved mind, the unholy mind, and the unbridled mind, must all be acknowledged as wrong sinful patterns, and repentance is necessary to rid the mind of these sinful patterns.

B. The repentance of sinful thought patterns

We often repent of sinful actions because they are seen and get us into trouble. But have you ever repented of sinful thought patterns? We often have to apologize for yelling at our children because we didn't deal with the anger that was welling up in our hearts. Repenting of the patterns of selfishness, pride, bitterness, unforgiveness, covetousness, jealousy, envy, and lust will save you from dealing with sinful actions later. *"For as he thinketh in his heart, so is he…"* (Proverbs 23:7).

Illustration

There was a commercial on television years ago for Fram oil filters. It showed an auto mechanic looking under the hood of a car with a smoking engine. Someone had failed to change his oil regularly and now his engine needed to be replaced—a very expensive proposition. The old mechanic would hold up the advertised oil filter and say, "You can pay me now, or you can pay me later." Repenting of sinful patterns is a price that must be paid now or we will pay dearly later.

II. Resist with Spirit-Filled Power

A. *The enhancement of the Spirit*

"And be renewed in the spirit of your mind" (Ephesians 4:23). The human spirit fails unless the Holy Spirit fills. D.L. Moody said, "God commands us to be filled with the Spirit; and if we aren't filled, it's because we are living beneath our privileges." You and I are not going to win this battle of our minds without the power of the Holy Spirit. As long as we think that we can think right on our own, we think wrong! *"…This is the word of the LORD unto Zerubbabel, saying, Not by might, nor by power, but by my spirit, saith the LORD of hosts"* (Zechariah 4:6).

"Now unto him that is able to do exceeding abundantly above all that we ask or think, according to the power that worketh in us" (Ephesians 3:20).

B. The emptying of self

Now in order to be filled, I must be empty. The gas tank on my car is always full. But while it is always full, I may come to a complete stop along the side of the road because of a lack of fuel. Let me explain: My tank is always full of something—either air or gasoline. Unfortunately, cars do not run on air, so we must keep them filled with fuel. When you put gasoline into your car, you are forcing the air in that tank out. This same principle applies to our lives. When we are filled with self, the Holy Spirit is forced out. But when we empty ourselves of self and the sinful patterns that accompany our sinful lives and we are filled with the Spirit of God, we will have thoughts and actions that are pleasing to God. John put it succinctly, *"He must increase, but I must decrease"* (John 3:30).

The analogy that the Bible uses in Ephesians 5 is interesting. *"And be not drunk with wine, wherein is excess; but be filled with the Spirit"* (Ephesians 5:18). When a person is drunk with alcohol, there is no question that he is "under the influence" of that which he has placed within him. He may try to cover up that influence, but he can't. Ask him to walk a straight line—he can't. Ask him to repeat the alphabet—he can't. His words are slurred, his mind is slowed, his movements are awkward, all because he cannot control himself. He is under the control of something else.

When we are empty of our own sinful patterns of thought and our minds are controlled by the Holy Spirit, it will likewise be undeniable. We can't hide it. It's obvious as our speech, our actions, and even our reactions are now controlled by the Spirit of God rather than our sinful flesh. Have you **Repented of Sinful Patterns** and are you **Resisting with Spirit-filled Power**? Martin Luther said that God made the world out of nothing, and it is only when we become nothing that God can make something out of us.

III. Replace with Scriptural Precepts

A. Putting off is equivalent to repentance.

"And that ye put on the new man, which after God is created in righteousness and true holiness" (Ephesians 4:24). The "replacement theory" as I like to call it, is found throughout the Bible. Putting off, that is repentance, is a huge first step in the process, but the wrong must be replaced by that which is right if victory is to be secured.

> **TEACHING TIP**
>
> *Consider reading these portions of Scripture out loud in class responsively, commenting on them in between references.*

Notice several places where God emphasizes replacement:

PSALM 1:1–2

1   *Blessed is the man that walketh not in the counsel of the ungodly, nor standeth in the way of sinners, nor sitteth in the seat of the scornful.*

2   *But his delight is in the law of the LORD; and in his law doth he meditate day and night.*

EPHESIANS 4:28

28   Let him that stole steal no more: but rather let him labour, working with his hands the thing which is good, that he may have to give to him that needeth.

ROMANS 12:9–21

9   Let love be without dissimulation. Abhor that which is evil; cleave to that which is good.

10   Be kindly affectioned one to another with brotherly love; in honour preferring one another;

11   Not slothful in business; fervent in spirit; serving the Lord;

12   Rejoicing in hope; patient in tribulation; continuing instant in prayer;

13   Distributing to the necessity of saints; given to hospitality.

14   Bless them which persecute you: bless, and curse not.

15   Rejoice with them that do rejoice, and weep with them that weep.

16   Be of the same mind one toward another. Mind not high things, but condescend to men of low estate. Be not wise in your own conceits.

17   Recompense to no man evil for evil. Provide things honest in the sight of all men.

18   If it be possible, as much as lieth in you, live peaceably with all men.

19   Dearly beloved, avenge not yourselves, but rather give place unto wrath: for it is written, Vengeance is mine; I will repay, saith the Lord.

20   Therefore if thine enemy hunger, feed him; if he thirst, give him drink: for in so doing thou shalt heap coals of fire on his head.

21   Be not overcome of evil, but overcome evil with good.

LESSON ELEVEN—THE CONFORMED MIND

B. Putting on is equivalent to restoration.

Paul sums it up nicely later, *"But now ye also put off all these; anger, wrath, malice, blasphemy, filthy communication out of your mouth. Lie not one to another, seeing that ye have put off the old man with his deeds; And have put on the new man, which is renewed in knowledge after the image of him that created him"* (Colossians 3:8–10). The old simply must be replaced by the new!

You say, "But I've been thinking wrong for so long; I just don't think I can change the way I think. I've tried to quit the wrong thought patterns. I've been to the altar and confessed them. They just keep coming back." Let's try an experiment. Think of the number *8*. Do you have it on your brain? Think about its shape. Think of a snowman, the 8-ball on a pool table, a V-8 drink, etc. Eight is a beautiful number isn't it? Now try to forget it. Stop thinking about an 8; erase it from your mind; don't think of its shape, or the amount for which it stands. Repent of the number 8! You can't do it, can you? The more you try to forget the 8, the more it's there. The same is true of a sinful thought. The more you focus on repenting of it, the harder it is to put it off.

Try this: Think of the number *100*. Add 4 to it; subtract 14 from it; divide it by 3; add 20; multiply it by 2; and then subtract 99. Did you think of that other number during that little sequence? You shouldn't have. (You should have the number *1* on your mind right now.) You will never rid your mind of sinful thoughts by focusing on how important it is to get rid of them. You must "replace" those thoughts. *"And the peace of God, which passeth all understanding, shall keep your hearts and minds through Christ Jesus. Finally, brethren, whatsoever things are true, whatsoever things are honest, whatsoever things are just,*

141

whatsoever things are pure, whatsoever things are lovely, whatsoever things are of good report; if there be any virtue, and if there be any praise, **think on these things.** *Those things, which ye have both learned, and received, and heard, and seen in me, do: and the God of peace shall be with you"* [Emphasis mine] (Philippians 4:7–9).

Your mind is a lot like the desktop of your computer. Whatever you leave on that desktop will be staring you in the face every time you log on. But if you will take the time to click on those unwanted items and drag them over to your "recycle bin" or "trash can," you won't remember that they are on your computer. Now to be sure, they are still in your computer, and you can find them (or your server can) if you go digging in the trash can, but if they are "out of sight," they are "out of mind."

When we continually feed our minds the wrong data day after day, is it any wonder we struggle with the same sinful thought patterns that lead us into sinful actions? Why don't you "click" on those wrong thoughts today and drag them under the blood of Christ? *"If we confess our sins, he is faithful and just to forgive us our sins, and to cleanse us from all unrighteousness"* (1 John 1:9). But don't stop there! Replace those wrong thoughts with right thoughts.

After confessing your sins first thing each morning, go ahead and put something on the desktop of your mind that will help you to think right and do right. Reading Scripture is a great start. Why not try memorizing a verse? Sing a hymn? Repeat a quote from last Sunday's sermon? Think about five people who have serious needs and pray for them. After a few of these disciplines to start your day, you won't be thinking about your "number 8" any more, and with time you'll forget about it altogether because your mind has been "renewed" through **Repentance, Resistance,** and **Replacement.**

Study Questions

1. What are we to do with our wickedness according to Acts 8:22?
   According to Acts 8:22, we are to repent of our wickedness.

2. List three or four sinful thought patterns that could threaten your life's direction.
   Answers may vary.

3. What analogy does the Scripture use in Ephesians 5:18? Expound upon the truth found in this verse.
   Ephesians 5:18 uses the analogy of being drunk with wine and being filled with the Spirit. When a person is drunk with alcohol, there is no question that he is "under the influence" of that which he has placed within him. He is under the control of something else. When we are empty of our own sinful patterns and are controlled by the Holy Spirit, we too will be undeniably controlled by Someone else.

4. The replacement theory—putting off the sinful nature and putting on a Spirit-filled life—is found throughout the Bible. God emphasizes "replacement" in several places throughout Scripture. Read the following Scriptures and summarize each replacement that was made: Psalm 1:1–2, Ephesians 4:28, and Romans 12:9–21.
   In Psalm 1:1–2, a man is blessed and happy if he does not walk in ungodly counsel but walks in the Law of the Lord. In Ephesians 4:28, instead of stealing, a challenge is made to labor. To summarize Romans 12:9–21, we ought to cleave to that which is good and hate evil. We are to be fervent and not lazy, be honest and not conceited, be peaceable and not revengeful, and we are to overcome evil with good.

143

5. The old must be replaced by that which is new. Write out Colossians 3:8–10.
    "But now ye also put off all these; anger, wrath, malice, blasphemy, filthy communication out of your mouth. Lie not one to another, seeing that ye have put off the old man with his deeds; And have put on the new man, which is renewed in knowledge after the image of him that created him:" (Colossians 3:8–10).

6. We cannot conform our minds to the mind of Christ in our own power. Read 2 Corinthians 3:5 and explain where we can get strength sufficient enough for this task.
    Conforming our minds to the mind of Christ requires the sufficiency of God according to 2 Corinthians 3:5.

7. List the three practical steps given in this lesson which lead to a mind conformed to Christ.
    The three practical steps that lead to a mind conformed to Christ are to repent of sinful patterns, resist with Spirit-filled power, and replace with scriptural precepts.

8. "Unless we have within us that which is above us, we will soon give in to the pressures around us." How can this quote help you live out your regular schedule this week?
    Answers may vary.

Memory Verse

"Not that we are sufficient of ourselves to think any thing as of ourselves; but our sufficiency is of God;"—2 CORINTHIANS 3:5

The Christ-Like Mind

Key Verses

PHILIPPIANS 2:5–8

5   Let this mind be in you, which was also in Christ Jesus:

6   Who, being in the form of God, thought it not robbery to be equal with God:

7   But made himself of no reputation, and took upon him the form of a servant, and was made in the likeness of men:

8   And being found in fashion as a man, he humbled himself, and became obedient unto death, even the death of the cross.

Lesson Summary

A recent trend started with the question, "What would Jesus do?" but this study encourages students to ask, "What would Jesus think?" In the last lesson, we learned to conform our minds to Christ's, and in this lesson, we are going to learn how to use our conformed minds by developing the characteristics of a Christ-like mind.

Lesson Aim

To challenge each student to get their thoughts out of the way by developing the mind of Christ.

Lesson Goals

At the conclusion of this lesson, students should:

1. Practice selflessness by making themselves "of no reputation."
2. Choose not to be filled with thoughts of only themselves.
3. Strive to live by the thought in Philippians 3:10, "That I may know him...."
4. Realize that the greatest goal they can have for their lives is to be a servant.
5. Submit to do anything that God asks them to do.

Teaching Outline

I. A Mind of Selflessness
   A. The ladder of no reputation
   B. The lesson of narcissistic regard

II. A Mind of Service
   A. The great servant
   B. A genuine service

III. A Mind of Submission
   A. The mind of Christ is to submit.
   B. The mind of Christ is by the Spirit.

The Christ-Like Mind

Text

EPHESIANS 4:20–21

20 But ye have not so learned Christ;

21 If so be that ye have heard him, and have been taught by him, as the truth is in Jesus:

Introduction

When we get *our* thoughts out of the way, we can then develop the mind of Christ. *"But ye have not so learned Christ; If so be that the ye have heard him, and have been taught by him, as the truth is in Jesus"* (Ephesians 4:20–21). There used to be a popular phrase that seemed to be everywhere. It was "What would Jesus do?" Many abbreviated it to WWJD. I'm sure this served as a good reminder to people who would see it printed somewhere or engraved on a bracelet to think about their actions. But prior to that we need to ask WWJT! (What Would Jesus Think?)

It would be remiss to study the subject of our minds without studying the words of Paul to the Philippians in chapter 2, *"Let this mind be in you, which was also in Christ Jesus: Who, being in the form of God, thought it not robbery to be equal with God: But made himself of no reputation, and took upon him the form of a servant, and was made in the likeness of men: And being found in fashion as a man, he humbled himself, and became obedient unto death, even the death of the cross"* (Philippians 2:5–8). What are the characteristics of a Christ-like mind?

I.   A Mind of Selflessness

A. The ladder of no reputation

Jesus Christ is God! He always has been and always will be. He *"thought it not robbery to be equal with God"* because He is God. When Jesus Christ claimed to be God, many thought He was blasphemous and plotted to kill Him, but He was merely telling the truth. *"In the beginning was the Word, and the Word was with God, and the Word was God"* (John 1:1). But Jesus Christ, God in the flesh, *"made himself of no reputation"* (Philippians 2:7A). What a contrast to the "climb the ladder of success" syndrome that exists today. Man is constantly padding his resume and adding to his credentials. Young people cheat to achieve grades worthy of a scholarship. Adults lie about their past and do whatever it takes to appear smarter, younger (or older), and more experienced, because after all, "perception is reality."

Standing between us and eternal success is self! We are our own worst enemy. D.L. Moody said, "The man

I fear the most is the one who walks underneath this hat." When Abraham Lincoln was running for president of the United States, a reporter asked him if he feared any of his opponents. Lincoln thought for a moment and responded, "Yes, one." The reporter was surprised since he was doing very well in the polls. He said, "Really, which one do you fear?" Lincoln said, "I fear a man named Lincoln. If I am defeated in this election, it will be by a man named Lincoln."

B. The lesson of narcissistic regard

Second Timothy 3:1 says, *"This know also, that in the last days perilous times shall come."* You might think: these must be the last days because they sure seem to be perilous. Who would have thought that we would be dealing with the problems of our society? Wars, political corruption, crime, gangs, immorality, etc. are in the headlines on a daily basis. It seems that *"evil men and seducers"* are waxing worse and worse.

But then, in 2 Timothy 3:2 the Bible says, *"For men shall be lovers of their own selves."* When I read this, it was like the Holy Spirit took a dagger and plunged it into my chest. When God defines the last days, He does not speak of crime, or war, or same gender marriages. The last days will be characterized by selfishness!

Perhaps the greatest compliment ever given to the Lord Jesus Christ was given by Paul who said, *"For even Christ pleased not himself"* (Romans 15:3A). Not one single day of His eternal existence was ever lived for Himself, for He said, *"And he that sent me is with me: the Father hath not left me alone; I do always those things that please him"* (John 8:29). How much of the last twenty-four hours did we spend pleasing Him? The honest truth is, we are often characterized by, *"For all seek their own, not the things which are Jesus Christ's"* (Philippians 2:21).

No one is so empty as the man who is filled with thoughts of only himself. God sends no one away empty except for the people who are filled with themselves.

Bob Zuppke, a famous football coach, once asked the question, "What makes a man fight?" He answered his own question by saying, "Two forces are at war in every fighter, the ego and the goal. An overdose of self-love, coddling of the ego, makes bums of men who ought to be champions. Forgetfulness of self, complete absorption in the goal often makes champions out of bums" (Charles L. Allen, *Joyful Living in the Fourth Dimension,* Baker Book House Company, 1983).

Remember, our goal is to become like Christ. The Apostle Paul was absorbed with that goal, *"That I may know him, and the power of his resurrection, and the fellowship of his sufferings, being made conformable unto his death"* (Philippians 3:10).

II. A Mind of Service

A. The great servant

"...and took upon him the form of a servant, and was made in the likeness of men" (Philippians 2:7B). *"For ye know the grace of our Lord Jesus Christ, that, though he was rich, yet for your sakes he became poor, that ye through his poverty might be rich"* (2 Corinthians 8:9). Jesus Christ, as God, left His throne in Heaven, wrapped Himself in flesh, and came to this sin-cursed world to serve! *"Even as the Son of man came not to be ministered unto, but to minister, and to give his life a ransom for many"* (Matthew 20:28).

Illustration

My cousin, my sister, and I were playing outside one day when I was a small boy. The two of them were three years older than I was and were talking about what they wanted to be when they got big. Finally, they decided to ask me. They said, "Hey John, what do you want to be when you get big?" I wasn't very smart then (I'm still not). I responded, "I want to be a fire truck." Obviously at that young age, I didn't know the difference between a fire truck and a fireman. Later, they decided to get another laugh, and so they asked me again about my goal in life. I decided to change my answer since they embarrassed me the last time. I said, "I want to be a hospital." They laughed even louder as I apparently didn't know the difference between a hospital and a doctor.

As I was growing up, there were many things I thought about doing. Once, as a teenager, I thought I wanted to be a barber, but that was back in the 1960s when no one was getting their hair cut. I decided that would be a dumb idea! Did you know that the greatest goal we could have for our lives is to be a servant? We are to have Christ's mind, and His mind was to serve. I tell our college students often that when they graduate, they ought to go out and find the lowest rung on the ladder. In a world where everyone is climbing the ladder of success, there won't be much competition for that bottom rung. Grab that place of lowly service and hang on, because one day God is going to turn the ladder around! *"For whosoever exalteth himself shall be abased; and he that humbleth himself shall be exalted"* (Luke 14:11).

B. A genuine service

Albert Einstein declared, "It is high time that the ideal of success should be replaced by the ideal of service." Too many people spell service, "serve us." Someone has said that the best exercise for our hearts is to bend down several times a day to help someone else. You say, "I don't have any talent or ability." God is not looking for ability; He's looking for availability, pliability, and dependability. The back porch light can do something the sun cannot—shine at night! God didn't save you to sit, soak, and sour. He saved you to stand, strive, and serve.

By the way, that's where the joy of the Christian life is found—in serving. The songwriter wrote, "There is joy in serving Jesus." That is exactly what Jesus taught, "*If ye know these things, happy are ye if ye do them*" (John 13:17). Jesus doesn't promise joy to those who simply *know* the Bible. He promises joy to those who *do* what they know. You can memorize all 31,000 verses in the Bible, but that won't make you happy. Karl Marx had Matthew, Mark, Luke, and John memorized as a teenager and could recite them perfectly in public, but he died an atheist.

> **TEACHING TIP**
>
> *Brainstorm with your class and make a list of how you can practice selflessness and service this week. Be as specific as possible.*

Illustration

Years ago, I was preaching a revival meeting in a small town in Wyoming. One of the men in the church would faithfully preach in the nursing home across the street on Sunday afternoons. After the Sunday services, he thought,

"Some of those people would enjoy these special services if I would bring them." Every night, he would arrive early, go across the street, and bring a number of those people over to the church in their wheelchairs.

On Tuesday night he brought a woman who did not appear to be extremely old, but was paralyzed from her waist down. He parked her in the center aisle about half-way back next to his family. She listened intently to the message and at the invitation time, looked up at the man who had brought her and said, "I want to go up there." He unlocked the brake on her chair and wheeled her forward. Upon arriving at the front, she told the pastor that she wanted to be saved, and several moments later was led to Christ by one of the women in the church.

She returned the next evening and on her way out, after shaking my hand, she said to the pastor, "Pastor, I got saved last night and now I know that I need to be baptized. Would you be able to baptize me?" He said, "Ma'am I would be delighted to baptize you. Here in our church we baptize on Sunday nights and if you could come this next Sunday night and give your testimony to one of our deacons, we could baptize you. Would that work out for you?" She said, "That would be great, but...." The pastor said, "Don't worry about a thing. I will get a couple of the deacons to help me and we will carry you down into the baptistery in your wheelchair. Then I will baptize you right in your chair. How does that sound?" She said, "Pastor, that would be wonderful!" Then she paused and said, "Pastor, after I get baptized and join the church, I want to work in the nursery." I thought to myself, "you've got to be kidding!" I mean, I know of people who ended up in wheelchairs *because of* working in the nursery, but she was already in one!

I guess the pastor must have had the same puzzled look on his face, because she pointed her finger up at him and said, "You don't think I'm too decrepit do you?" He said, "Oh no, not at all; we'll get you in there." Don't you love that spirit? No one would have thought any less of this woman if all she did was come to church, but God had done something in her life and now she wanted to serve Him. Do you have that mind to serve? It's the mind of Christ.

Illustration

Be careful, because if you tell God you're willing to serve Him, He will more than likely give you a chance to prove it. In our ministry, our pastor has taught us to greet people and say, "Is there anything I can do for you?" It sounds great, is quite impressive, but becomes very routine. We say it to the UPS man who delivers packages, to first-time visitors in church, to prospective students, to anyone who dares step foot on our campus. We don't really mean it; we just say it!

A few years back, an elderly lady in our church had become ill and was hospitalized. Reports were coming back that she may not have long to live. I had met this couple years ago in a revival meeting in California. The man had a great solo voice and used to sing in revival meetings where I would preach. They were a delightful couple and I was thrilled to catch up with them when I started preaching revival meetings at the Lancaster Baptist Church in 1986. When I assumed my position with the college, I was excited to see them more often and enjoyed their friendship and fellowship. Now she was perhaps on her deathbed and I knew that I needed to go up and see them. But good intentions got eaten up by to-do lists and

I kept putting it off. I knew that I would deeply regret not going up and having prayer with them if she should slip into eternity.

One day as I finished my last class around 1:00 PM, I decided that everything else was going to have to wait. I jumped in my car and headed for the hospital. Calling back to my office, I informed my secretary that I would be back on campus in an hour—I was headed to the hospital. Upon entering the room, I went over to the bedside and offered some words of encouragement, read some Scripture, and prayed. This wonderful servant of Christ for many years, smiled, thanked me and drifted back to sleep.

I sat down with her husband and we talked for about forty minutes about various things including the funeral that he wanted for his dear wife. I glanced at my watch—it was ten minutes until two. I said, "I need to be getting back to the office. Let me have a word of prayer with you." We bowed our heads and prayed and when I finished, I stood up and said, "I've got to be going; It was great to visit with you; I'll be praying for you; *Is there anything I can do for you?*"

He stood up and said, "Yes, there is!" I was stunned. No one had ever responded this way before. Pastor Chappell had not taught us—as far as I could remember—what to say next. So, I said, "What is it?" He exclaimed, "I want a pair of shoes just like Pastor Chappell's." I said, "You do?" He said, "Yup, and I know you can get 'em for me." I said, "You mean the loafers with the little tassels on the top." "Those are the ones," he said. "What color?" I asked. He said, "Black." I asked "What size?" He said, "Seven." Heading for the door, I called back, "I'll be back in an hour."

I had a smile on my face and a spring in my step *until* I got to the hallway. Suddenly the smile and the spring was gone. My pace quickened to a frantic jog as I headed for the stairs and out to my car. "A pair of shoes! Lord, what's this all about? I don't have time to buy a pair of shoes! Do I look like a shopper? I scanned my brain for the nearest store that might have a pair of shoes. There was a Marshall's store about a mile away. I raced to the store praying that God would let me find them quickly. Marshalls didn't have them. I headed to Mervyns a few blocks further down the street. No luck. I was learning now that size seven was a very small size for a man's shoe! Both of these stores had informed me that they did not carry any men's shoes in a size seven, much less the kind I was looking for.

I thought, I'm going to have to go to the mall! I hate the mall! Making my way down the freeway, I pulled into the parking lot and ran to the first "normal" store—J.C. Penney. Then to Sears, then to Gottschalks—I was working my way up. Finally, there was only one store left: Dillards! Second cousin to Macys. I never shop there except during the January sale. They had them! Just like Pastor Chappell's; in black; and size seven. I picked them up and turned them over to see the price: $129.95!

I didn't have that kind of cash on me, but I did possess a credit card, so I bought the shoes.

About an hour after I had left, I walked back into that hospital room with a box of shoes. I said, "There you go—just like Pastor Chappell's." He said, "Thank you." I said, "You're welcome" and walked out. You know, I've never seen that man wear those shoes! Oh, I look every time I see him. As I shake his hand, I'm pulling up his trousers with the other hand. To this day I have no idea why he wanted those shoes, but I know why God had me go and get them. God taught me an important lesson that day about serving. It's one thing to sing the songs about serving and talk the talk. It's quite another matter to walk the walk! It took me a while to pay off the price of those shoes, but it was a joy to do so because God had given me a chance to serve!

> **TEACHING TIP**
>
> *Tell of a time when you served someone else although it inconvenienced you. Talk about the joy you received from being a servant.*

III. A Mind of Submission

A. The mind of Christ is to submit.

"*And being found in fashion as a man, he humbled himself, and became obedient unto death, even the death of the cross*" (Philippians 2:8). From a very early age, man seems to think that the ideal is to be autonomous rather than submissive. But the mind of Christ is to submit.

"*…My meat is to do the will of him that sent me, and to finish his work*" (John 4:34). "*He went away again the second time, and prayed, saying, O my Father, if this cup may not pass away from me, except I drink it, thy will be done*" (Matthew 26:42).

Are you willing to do anything that God asks you to do? Is there anything that you are unwilling to do?

> **Illustration**

Soon after we were married, my wife Diane and I joined a Baptist church that was growing and exciting. While

157

we were on the road in evangelism most weeks during the year, we always enjoyed coming home to our church and being as much a part as we could. The pastor and his family became dear friends as did many of the couples in that church. But trouble came. Soon we were losing people, and all kinds of rumors began to circulate—none of which turned out to be true. I was restless. As an evangelist, I could choose to live wherever I wanted. I wanted to be a part of a strong church, and I was tempted to leave that struggling situation.

On a particular Wednesday night during the song service, we were singing the song, "I'll go where you want me to go, dear Lord." After the first verse, our pastor who had founded that church and had faithfully served for nearly twenty-five years, interrupted the song leader and said, "When we get to the chorus on this next verse, let's sing, 'I'll stay where you want me to stay, dear Lord.'" The Holy Spirit struck the dagger to my heart once again that night. It would have been easy to "go" anywhere, but there at that moment, the Holy Spirit wanted me to submit and "stay." You don't soon forget those lessons.

B. The mind of Christ is by the Spirit.

Our critics often say that as Christians we are under some kind of "mind control." I plead guilty. Paul said, "…we have the mind of Christ" (1 Corinthians 2:16B). Wouldn't you much rather have the mind of Christ than the mind of the flesh or the mind of the world? "For they that are after the flesh do mind the things of the flesh; but they that are after the Spirit the things of the Spirit. For to be carnally minded is death; but to be spiritually minded is life and peace" (Romans 8:5–6). "Forasmuch then as Christ hath suffered for us in the *flesh, arm yourselves likewise with the same mind: for he that hath suffered in the flesh hath ceased from sin; That he no longer should live the rest of his time in the flesh to the lusts of men, but to the will of God"* (1 Peter 4:1–2).

Conclusion

How will you choose to live the rest of your time? In the lust of your flesh or with the mind of Christ?

Illustration

Years ago, I was privileged to speak at a summer camp for teenagers with Dr. Ed Nelson, long time pastor and educator. In one of his messages, he told how one day he and his wife were walking down the street to a restaurant in Denver, Colorado when they spotted the headline of the newspaper in a vending machine. The headline read: **LUCY DIES!** Dr. Nelson looked at his wife and said, "Who's Lucy?" She didn't know either, and so upon sitting down to eat they asked the waitress who Lucy was. She said Lucille Ball from "I Love Lucy." Dr. Nelson and his wife looked at each other and shrugged. Neither of them had ever heard of Lucille Ball or the famous television program.

I thought to myself, "that's impossible." Everybody in that era had heard of "I Love Lucy." But not the Nelsons. He went on to explain that he and his wife had never watched a single moment of television in their entire lives up to that point. I was stunned! Not even the news? The World Series? The Super Bowl? Nothing?

As I contemplated that later, I thought, "What have they missed?" The answer—not much! Their minds and hearts were not cluttered with non-essential things. (Not to mention the countless temptations to sin that they were never exposed to either.) Their lifetime of ministry was testimony to their minds being filled with the things that are true, honest, just, pure, lovely, of good report, virtuous, and praiseworthy. We have the same choice.

Study Questions

1. God wants us to have selfless minds. However, when you read Romans 1:25, does this verse describe your Christianity? Explain your answer.
    Answers may vary.

2. The greatest goal we could have for our lives is to be a servant. We are to have Christ's mind, and His mind is to serve. How can you serve God's people this week? In what ways can you serve more this week than you did last week?
    Answers may vary.

3. Are you willing to do anything that God asks you to do? Is there anything that you are unwilling to do?
    Answers may vary.

4. P.T. Forsyth said, "The purpose in life is not to find your freedom, but your Master." Give five reasons that show how you are living a life that is directed to becoming more like your Master. (Example: (1) I memorize Scripture to have the mind of Christ.)
    Answers may vary.

5. When we get "our thoughts" out of the way, we can then develop the mind of Christ. Write out Ephesians 4:20–21.
    "But ye have not so learned Christ; If so be that ye have heard him, and have been taught by him, as the truth is in Jesus:"—Ephesians 4:20–21

6. According to Romans 15:3, not one single day of Jesus' eternal existence was ever lived for Himself. What did He live for according to John 8:29?
    Jesus lived for the task of always doing those things that pleased His Father, according to John 8:29.

7. After reading 2 Timothy 3:2, what does *"For men shall be lovers of their own selves"* mean?
    "For men shall be lovers of their own selves" means that men will be selfish as described in 2 Timothy 3:2.

8. How will you choose to live the rest of your life? Will you live in the lust of your flesh or with the mind of Christ? Read Romans 8:5–6 and 1 Peter 4:1–2.
    Answers may vary.

Memory Verses

"Let this mind be in you, which was also in Christ Jesus: Who, being in the form of God, thought it not robbery to be equal with God: But made himself of no reputation, and took upon him the form of a servant, and was made in the likeness of men: And being found in fashion as a man, he humbled himself, and became obedient unto death, even the death of the cross."
—PHILIPPIANS 2:5–8

The Committed Mind

Key Verse

PSALM 119:11

11 *Thy word have I hid in mine heart, that I might not sin against thee.*

Lesson Summary

Who doesn't want to be successful? If each person had the choice to live a meaningless life or a life overflowing with success, I guarantee that each one would choose to succeed hands down! Success is coveted, worked for, sought after, and for most, a distant dream. However, success comes from the one source that we have been studying—it's obtainable! According to Joshua 1:8, it comes as a result of "meditating" on God's Word, and we can't meditate on something that we haven't put in our hearts! This lesson concludes this study on the mind by showing the importance of Scripture memory and by giving practical steps on how every person can fruitfully memorize Scripture with a committed mind.

Lesson Aim

To encourage students to implement Scripture memory into their lives.

Lesson Goals

At the conclusion of this lesson, students should:

1. Understand that knowing God's Word will help them when faced with Satan's temptations.
2. Thoroughly engage in the six steps of Scripture memory—putting them into practice right away.
3. Choose a definite time and place for Scripture memory.
4. Decide on a topic and write out 3x5 cards containing correlating verses and their references.
5. Grasp the wonderful reality that hiding God's Word in their hearts pleases God.

Teaching Outline

I. The Important Start
   A. Specify a point in time.
   B. Specify a place to try.

II. The Inclusive Systematizing
   A. Consider the Teacher.
   B. Choose a topic.

III. The Intent of Sound
   A. The reason to be audible
   B. The reward to the applicable

IV. The Interesting Shift
   A. The body's rhythm
   B. The body's routine

V. The Intense Study
   A. The will to review
   B. The work to review

VI. The Intent Set
   A. The goal of a moment
   B. The gratitude of memorizing

The Committed Mind

Text

DEUTERONOMY 6:6, 11:8

6   *And these words, which I command thee this day, shall be in thine heart:*

8   *Therefore shall ye keep all the commandments which I command you this day, that ye may be strong, and go in and possess the land, whither ye go to possess it;*

PSALM 119:11

11   *Thy word have I hid in mine heart, that I might not sin against thee.*

ROMANS 10:8

8   *But what saith it? The word is nigh thee, even in thy mouth, and in thy heart: that is, the word of faith, which we preach;*

COLOSSIANS 3:16

16   *Let the word of Christ dwell in you richly in all wisdom; teaching and admonishing one another in psalms and hymns and spiritual songs, singing with grace in your hearts to the Lord.*

Introduction

Illustration

Often people come up to me after I preach and say, "My, you have a wonderful memory. I wish I could memorize like that! God has really gifted you with a great mind." I want to cry! Now don't misunderstand. I am what I am by the grace of God (1 Corinthians 15:10)! Paul said, *"For who maketh thee to differ from another? and what hast thou that thou didst not receive? now if thou didst receive it, why dost thou glory, as if thou hadst not received it?"* (1 Corinthians 4:7).

Usually, I respond to those comments with, "Well, I have a photographic mind, but I ran out of film a couple of years ago." They laugh, and that's the end of the conversation.

But before we continue, let me share with you the real secret to memorizing Scripture—time and work. Now, don't stop listening, because in the next few minutes, we can see how to make that *time* effective and the *work* enjoyable.

Let me tell you how it all started with me. When I was in college, I decided after an enjoyable freshman speech class to minor in the subject. I did it because I thought it would be fun, not because I thought I would ever use anything I was about to learn. Because of that minor in speech, I was required to participate in the college dramas that were performed on campus twice each year, as well as recite poetry and monologues in various services. I was also required to be in a recital at the end of my senior year. This called for a lot of memorizing. I was in the plays *As You Like It, Hamlet, The Robe, Julius Caesar,* and my favorite—*Cyrano*! My German nose helped me land that part! In *Cyrano* alone, I had over 1,500 lines to memorize, and I also had to know *when* to say them, so I had to memorize the lines just before mine too! For my recital, I did the comedy, *Teahouse of the August Moon.* I loved it and would do it all again if I had the chance.

By the time graduation rolled around, my brain was fried! It couldn't hold any more "memory," and so for the next four years, I did not conscientiously memorize anything! But, I was always convicted that I should. I would listen to preachers quote portions of Scripture and think, I could do that. I was busy in revival work: writing sermons, preaching, winning souls, helping churches, being a husband and dad, etc., and so excused myself from any further discipline in the "study" area. But the Holy Spirit kept reminding me, "If you could memorize Shakespeare—you could memorize Scripture."

In October of 1978, we were holding a Christian school revival in Coleman, Wisconsin. I preached several times during the school day to various age groups, but there were no services or activities in the evening. The town of Coleman at that time had a population of three hundred, and when five o'clock in the evening rolled around, the town shut down. Stores were not open, people disappeared from the streets, and everything became extremely quiet. I was bored to tears! My wife and I were traveling in a twenty-five-foot trailer. Our oldest son John, was just a little over a year old. The first night after supper, I went to the gym and shot some baskets for a couple of hours, but there's only so much fun you can have by yourself. Finally, after a couple of nights of this, I announced to Diane that I was going inside the school to memorize some Bible verses.

The only reason I did it was because I was bored and needed something to kill time. As I sat there that first night contemplating where to start, I realized that almost every week in revivals, I would preach a message on the subject of Hell. So, that's where I started. In the next couple of hours, I had memorized about ten verses on Hell and was pretty proud of myself. It was kind of fun to "preach" them as I would memorize them in the big gym that would make my voice sound more powerful than it was. I got so excited about it that the next night I went back inside and went at it again. By the end of that week, I had memorized about thirty verses on Hell, including the entire passage in Luke sixteen about the rich man and Lazarus.

I really didn't plan for it to go any further than that. I had killed some time with something profitable and knew that I would probably not have too many weeks when I would ever be that bored again. Our next revival was in Hadley, Michigan and when we arrived, the pastor informed me that Monday evening would be Awana Parent's Night and that several unsaved couples would be there to watch a short program and then I would preach. I was excited about the opportunity to preach to a good number of lost people (there were eighteen visiting couples there that night), and decided to preach on "Hell." But for the first time in my life, instead of reading the verses from the Bible in my message, I quoted them. I can't explain the power and life I felt in those words, which were not mine, but God's! For the first time in my ministry I felt like I was preaching "the Word."

I believe there were twelve adults who trusted Christ in that service! The next morning, I was up at 4:00 AM memorizing verses, and I've been hooked on the power of God's Word ever since. But long before I ever discovered this potential, God wrote, *"And these words, which I command thee this day, shall be **in thine heart**"* [Emphasis mine] (Deuteronomy 6:6). *"Therefore shall ye lay up these my words **in your heart and in your soul...**"* [Emphasis mine] (Deuteronomy 11:18). *"Thy word have I hid **in mine heart**, that I might not sin against thee"* [Emphasis mine] (Psalm 119:11). *"But what saith it? The word is nigh thee, even in thy mouth, and **in thy heart**: that is, the word of faith, which we preach"* [Emphasis mine] (Romans 10:8). *"Let the word of Christ **dwell in you** richly..."* [Emphasis mine] (Colossians 3:16).

Regardless of what this world teaches about success, God makes it clear that success only comes from one source, *"This book of the law shall not depart out of thy mouth; but thou shalt meditate therein day and night, that thou mayest observe to do according to all that is written therein: for then thou shalt make thy way prosperous, and then thou shalt have good success"* [Emphasis mine] (Joshua 1:8). This is the only time you will find the word *success* in the Bible, and God states that it comes as a result of "meditating" on His Word. You can't meditate on something you haven't put in your heart!

There are many good "plans" out there to help you memorize, but let me share with you what has worked for me. It's a little bit unique, but remember, "time and work" are the key. The biblical principle is "what you sow is what you reap" so you'll get out of this in exact proportion to the time and energy you put in to it.

I. The Important Start

A. *Specify a point in time.*

Very little gets accomplished in our lives that isn't planned. If you are seriously going to memorize Scripture, you must be willing to block off a section of time when you are free from other distractions of life. I'm not talking about your commute drive here or time in the check-out line at Wal-Mart! I'm talking about time like Jesus spent alone in communion with His Father: *"And in the morning, rising up a great while before day, he went out, and departed into a solitary place, and there prayed"* (Mark 1:35). *"And when he had sent the multitudes away, he went up into a mountain apart to pray: and when the evening was come, he was there alone"* (Matthew 14:23).

B. *Specify a place to try.*

Most of us today resist being "alone." We feel like we always have to be in the middle of the action. May I say that some of the loneliest people in the world are in the middle of a crowd. They are surrounded by people, but are lonely. There is a huge difference between loneliness and solitude. Solitude is something you choose, and you'd better, if you plan to survive in this world. We need time with God and His Word "alone"!

You say, "You don't understand my world. I'm surrounded by people from the time I get up until I go to bed. My time is never my own." And I say, that's why you're frustrated and about to "burn out"! In Mark 1, Jesus was surrounded by people (read His schedule beginning in verse 21!) But the next morning, while everyone else was still asleep, He chose a solitary place (verse 35). There is a time when no one else is up! You say, "But I'm not a morning person." You can become one. We're talking about success here rather than failure! Someone has said, "The difference between genius and average is what you do while everyone else is sleeping." Get up thirty minutes before everyone else does and see what a difference it will make in your spiritual life as you spend that time memorizing God's Word.

II. The Inclusive Systematizing

A. *Consider the Teacher.*

The purpose of memorization is to be able to recall Scripture when you need it, and for the purpose you need it. *"For he mightily convinced the Jews, and that publickly, shewing by the scriptures that Jesus was Christ"*

(Acts 18:28). The Bible covers hundreds of subjects, and it is through these topics that it applies to our lives. When Jesus was tempted by Satan in the wilderness (Matthew 4), He did not just throw out any old verse to overcome the temptation. He used specific Old Testament Scriptures that dealt with temptation. When Satan tempted Him to turn the stones into bread to ease His hunger, He quoted Deuteronomy 8:3, "...*It is written, Man shall not live by bread alone, but by every word that proceedeth out of the mouth of God*" (Matthew 4:4).

B. Choose a topic.

It may be an area of sin with which you are struggling like pride, worry, lust or selfishness. Get a concordance and look up that subject. You will find dozens of verses listed under the major topics of the Bible.

Get some cards and write the verses out on those "memory" cards. It doesn't matter what size you use—it depends on how good your eyes are. I used a small card about the size of a business card (a 4x6 index card cut into four equal parts). Writing the verses out on these cards is the first process of memorizing. I am aware that there are programs where you can buy the cards already printed. A pastor once asked me if he could photocopy my cards. I said, "Sure, but they'll never make it out of your desk drawer if you do." There is great value in writing the verses out in long hand. God commanded it to be done in the Old Testament.

DEUTERONOMY 6:9
9   *And thou shalt write them upon the posts of thy house, and on thy gates.*

DEUTERONOMY 17:18

18   And it shall be, when he sitteth upon the throne of his kingdom, that he shall write him a copy of this law in a book out of that which is before the priests the Levites.

DEUTERONOMY 27:3, 8

3   And thou shalt write upon them all the words of this law, when thou art passed over, that thou mayest go in unto the land which the LORD thy God giveth thee, a land that floweth with milk and honey; as the LORD God of thy fathers hath promised thee
8   And thou shalt write upon the stones all the words of this law very plainly.

In all of the sermon preparation, lecture notes, and writing that I have done over the years, I have never one time in my life, "cut and pasted" Scripture. Laugh if you want, but I just believe when God said to *"Study to shew thyself approved unto God..."* (2 Timothy 2:15). He wasn't thinking about "point and click," "cut and paste"! There is a disciplined process in memorization, and it starts with writing out the verses.

Now here is where my plan is a little different from others. When I decided to start memorizing seriously in 1978, I thought through how I was going to be using what I had memorized. I had two situations in my ministry when I most often needed to know the Bible—when I was preaching and when I was talking with people one-on-one in soulwinning or counseling. When I was preaching, I really didn't need to know the reference, because I could write that in my notes. I could write "Joshua 1:8." If I had memorized the verse, seeing that reference would trigger it in my mind, and I could quote it. But when I was talking with people personally, I really didn't need to know the verse, because I usually had my Bible with me and I could show them the verse (which is usually wise anyway in soulwinning), but I needed to know the reference so that I would know where to turn.

Most memory plans have cards with the reference on one side of the card and then you flip it over and the verse is written out on the reverse side. That's great, but it wasn't going to meet my need. So, I decided that I needed to memorize both the reference and the verse. I took my subject, such as "Hell," and found all of the verses in my concordance on that subject. I chose the ones I wanted to memorize and arranged them in chronological order (as they come in the Bible). This is already done in the concordance, but I chose to skip some and memorize others. I was now going to memorize that entire block of verses, in order as they come in the Bible, with both reference and the verse.

So, on the front of the card, I wrote "Hell #1" as illustrated below:

Front of the card:

Hell #1

When I flipped the card over, I wrote out the reference and the verse as illustrated:

Back of the card:

> **Psalm 9:17**
>
> The wicked shall be turned into hell, and all the nations that forget God.

As I memorized that subject, I memorized not only the verse but the reference with it. The first verse in that stack of cards then cued me to the second verse with its reference and text, and the second verse cued me to the third verse, etc. Thus, I memorized an entire block of verses together under one subject, all in order as they came in the Bible chronologically.

The second card in my series of verses on the subject of "Hell" looked like this:

Front of the card:

Hell #2

Back of the card:

> **Matthew 3:12**
>
> Whose fan is in his hand, and he will throughly purge his floor, and gather his wheat into the garner; but he will burn up the chaff with unquenchable fire.

This method creates a catalog of verses in your mind under various topics, and you are able to apply them to needs at any time. If you are struggling with a particular sin, when the temptation comes, you now have a series of verses to fire at the tempter. For the soulwinner, if someone you meet says, "Well, I don't believe in a place called Hell!" immediately, you know right where to take him in the Bible and show him the evidence of God's Word. For the preacher or teacher, as you are preparing a sermon or lesson, and the text you are preaching deals with a specific subject, immediately you have your own "mental concordance" on that subject from which to draw. (Here is where all that time you thought you were wasting by "writing and memorizing verses" is going to come back and save you hours of searching for just the right verse.) If you are memorizing more than one verse in a row (for example, let's say you are on the subject of "Hell" and you want to memorize Luke 16:19–31, which is the story of the rich man and Lazarus), on the front of the card, you put "Hell #8," or whatever number it is in your sequence. On the back you write "Luke 16:19–31." Get as many of the verses as you can on that first card and then start a second card. On the front of it you would put "Hell #8B" and continue the text on the back. If you need a third card, it would be "Hell #8C," and so on.

Now you have your stack of cards. You may have selected five or ten under a particular topic or hundreds; it all depends on how comprehensive you want to be. Just remember, you are doing this so you can use it, not just to see how many you can memorize. This isn't Vacation Bible School—there are no ribbons—but this is ministry, and there are great rewards!

Let's start memorizing. We have our tool, now let's make it work!

III. The Intent of Sound

A. The reason to be audible

Work out loud. This is why we have chosen a quiet place, alone. This is part of the process that works. You see, God emphasizes "hearing" His Word. *"But he said, Yea rather, blessed are they that hear the word of God and keep it"* (Luke 11:28). *"Therefore whosoever heareth these sayings of mine, and doeth them, I will liken him unto a wise man, which built his house upon a rock"* (Matthew 7:24). *"He that hath an ear, let him hear what the Spirit saith unto the churches"* (Revelation 3:22).

B. The reward to the applicable

You have read it and written it out; now you are "hearing it," as phrase by phrase you commit it to memory. Some verses are easier to memorize than others, so don't get frustrated. Keep going over phrases or words of the verse one at a time and then add more to it, always repeating all of it out loud. No secrets here—this takes time—but look at it as an investment. God said, *"For the merchandise of it is better than the merchandise of silver, and the gain thereof than fine gold. She is more precious than rubies: and all the things thou canst desire are not to be compared unto her"* (Proverbs 3:14–15). He adds in verse 18, *"...and happy is every one that retaineth her."*

IV. The Interesting Shift

A. The body's rhythm

Your body has rhythm. I'm sure you can tell who is coming down the hall of your house by their walk. Little children are able to memorize the words to songs long before they can read because the words are written to the rhythm of music. I can guarantee that you will memorize Scripture faster by walking than by sitting in a chair (or behind the wheel of your car stuck in rush hour traffic).

Illustration

I was preaching at a teen camp one summer. I came out of my room and there was a young girl about fifteen years old sitting on a rock with her Bible in her lap, and she was crying. I went over to her and asked her why she was crying. She said, "I've been trying to memorize this verse for the last thirty minutes and I just can't get it!" (She was trying to earn points for her team.) I took her Bible from her asking which verse it was that she was struggling with. I said, "Let me hear what you've got so far." Quite honestly, she didn't have much. She stammered through the first couple of words and got stuck. I must admit it was a rather difficult verse. I said, "Stand up." I pointed to a trailer about fifty yards down the sidewalk from where we were standing. "Take the Bible and walk toward that trailer and come back. Do exactly what you have been trying to do to memorize the verse while you walk. I'll wait for you right here and when you get back, we'll see how much you know." She looked at me like I was weird, but took off. She made it to the trailer and turned around. (I could see her lips moving as she was mouthing the words.) She got about ten feet from the trailer and began running toward me, yelling, "I've got it! I've got it!" Sure enough, she did too. Now granted, she had been working on it before my experiment, but the rhythm of her walk sealed it in her mind.

Try it—the exercise won't hurt you either.

B. The body's routine

I have been in small guest quarters at times and had only enough space to take three or four steps, turn around and walk back, but it makes all the difference in the world. The rhythm in your body will make the verse not only a part of your mind but also a part of your entire being. You will sense the power of God's Word as you use it in your life.

V. The Intense Study

A. The will to review

Repetition is the key to learning. Some memory plans will tell you that if you say the verse a certain number of times for a certain number of days, you'll never forget it. That doesn't seem to work for me. I have to keep reviewing every verse. I have often stated, "We've all had more than one telephone number in our lives, but we probably only remember the one we are using now." Use it or lose it, as they say. Until you have learned your entire stack of verses under a subject, you'll need to go through all of them every day. Once you have that whole topic memorized, you may be able to reduce your review of that subject to once a week. Perhaps later, less, but you'll have to keep going over them.

B. The work to review

I figured it out one day. For every verse I have memorized over these years, counting all of the time it took to write out the verse, the memorization time and the review time, I have spent two hundred hours on every verse that I have memorized! Now do you still think I have a photographic memory? I mean, really—I could teach a bad parrot to quote a verse in two hundred hours! Don't tell me you just can't memorize, or you're too old, or whatever. You can, but like I said, it takes time and work.

VI. The Intent Set

A. *The goal of a moment*
Once you start memorizing and using God's Word, you'll not be able to get verses written on cards fast enough. Let me caution you. Don't set a goal of how many verses you want to memorize in a day, week, month, or year. The truth is some passages are much easier to memorize than others. You are already familiar with them, or they are narrative or story-type in nature and thus the material flows very easily and logically. Others are not like that. The biblical wording is sometimes different than the way we might say it today, and the sentence might be compounded in nature. You might spend several days on one verse. You will get discouraged if you set your goals on the number of verses. Set a goal of the amount of "time" you are going to spend daily, weekly, monthly, on memorization. Commit yourself to that time no matter what; and as you do, the number of verses will add up over the months and years.

B. *The gratitude of memorizing*
In conclusion, let me say that some of the most enjoyable times of my life have been spent alone memorizing God's Word. In the wee hours of the morning, it's just God and me with His Word. Some might call it a sacrifice, but

WHAT'S ON YOUR MIND?

God went to a lot of trouble to give us His Word, and my effort to put it into my life seems pretty small in comparison. I have found that He has blessed that effort over these years.

Conclusion

Oh, how I have enjoyed seeing God use the Scripture that I have hidden in my heart. It has helped me in those moments of temptation, and I have had the joy of sharing it with countless others through preaching, teaching, counseling, and soulwinning. In Haggai 2:19a, God asks a question, *"Is the seed yet in the barn?"* In Luke 8:11, Jesus declared, *"The seed is the word of God."* Every spring my dad would buy seed corn. That seed never produced a harvest while in the bag stacked in the barn. We had to get it out into the field. That required a lot of time and effort, but once this was completed there was a great harvest. The seed of God's Word doesn't accomplish anything if it is left in the barn of a Book. But if you will take the time and effort to sow it in your heart now, you will enjoy a wonderful harvest.

> **TEACHING TIP**
>
> *Have 3x5 cards available at the end of class to help students get a jump start on Scripture memory. Give an incentive for next week to those who have written out a topic, verse, and have memorized it.*

Study Questions

1. In what verse of the Bible is the word *success* found?
   In Joshua 1:8, the word success is found.

2. The first step to memorizing Scripture is to choose a specific time and a quiet place. This week, write out when and where you can plan to memorize Scripture.
   Answers may vary.

3. The purpose of memorization is to be able to recall Scripture when you need it and for the purpose you need it. Decide today what topic of verses you would like to begin memorizing; list the topic and three verses to correlate with it (i.e., Topic: Prayer. Verses: Psalm 55:17, Mark 1:35, and Hebrews 4:16). Take one step further and write these verses out on 3x5 cards.
   Answers may vary.

4. What did Jesus use in response to Satan's temptation? Refer to Matthew 4:4 and Deuteronomy 8:3.
   In response to Satan's temptation (Matthew 4), Jesus quoted Deuteronomy 8:3—He used Scripture to fight off temptation.

5. Explain in your own words what the following verses have in common: Luke 11:28, Matthew 7:24, and Revelation 3:22
   The following verses: Luke 11:28, Matthew 7:24, and Revelation 3:22 all emphasize the "hearing" of God's Word.

6. Scripture memory takes both time and work. After hearing these words, many cringe and shy away from starting the process of memorization. If your life is busy already, consider giving up something on your schedule to set aside time to memorize God's Word. What is an area in your life that you can replace with time in God's Word?
    Answers may vary.

7. Read Colossians 3:16. What does God want to richly dwell in us?
    God wants the Word of Christ to richly dwell in us according to Colossians 3:16.

8. After learning the importance and practicality of Scripture memory, write out three reasons God would want you to memorize Scripture.
    Answers may vary.

Memory Verse

"This book of the law shall not depart out of thy mouth; but thou shalt meditate therein day and night, that thou mayest observe to do according to all that is written therein: for then thou shalt make thy way prosperous, and then thou shalt have good success."—JOSHUA 1:8

Striving Together
P u b l i c a t i o n s

For additional Christian
growth resources visit
www.strivingtogether.com

Pg. 29